CAPABLE OF BETRAYAL
A Survivor Takes Down the Phillips Exeter Academy Sex Predator
By
Michael Caven, MS

www.capableofbetrayal.com
www.michaelcaven.com
www.spillingthetea-memoir.com
www.outonmain.com

Dedicated to survivors everywhere.
May you find peace and happiness.
You certainly deserve both.
This is my love letter to you.

Michael Caven

CONTENTS

Michael Caven

Introduction

This memoir is about revisiting the past—especially the dark parts of our past that we don't usually want to revisit—so we can create a brighter future. In my case, I was a chameleon and shapeshifter for many years. I'd go into a metaphorical phone booth like Clark Kent and come out pretending to be whomever or whatever I thought I needed to be. I often wanted to be anything other than who I'd been told I was or should be.

Maybe you can relate.

The official starting point of this story is 1989. I was living in Dallas and had just received sexually explicit Polaroids of myself in the mail. I found myself thinking, *My god, who is that boy? Is he having fun? His eyes seem dazed.* I was drunk and high when the photos were taken, the amyl nitrite having lifted me out of my body. I'd lost myself, and now, again, I found myself wondering: *Who am I? How did I wind up here? What's next?*

My schoolteacher, Larry Lane Bateman, had mailed the photos to me, with dozens of pornographic videotapes. Bateman had helped many of his students "let their hair down," to reveal their inner actors and actresses on the North Shore High School Viking Masquers' stage. Seeing the photos prompted me to reinvent myself one more time—with the help of a therapist—to find the real me and get justice.

This story is also about the events in my childhood that made me vulnerable to a predator. And it's about intergenerational family dysfunction, abuse, addiction, recovery and relapse—an area I excelled in. My story is driven by impossible situations and seemingly impossible odds. More than anything, this book is about resilience. No matter how much humiliation, loss, or self-loathing you've experienced, this story promises a new beginning.

After being objectified by my teacher, and other male and female caregivers as a kid and teen, I found validation and hustled for drinks, drugs, and attention in Manhattan. I was a strutting little god making my way through notorious east side hustler bars, loving being wanted, needed, and adored. That was my self-worth.

This best self has been a long time coming. Along the way I've ruthlessly practiced what RuPaul calls *The Inner Saboteur.* My version: *The Inner Cannibal.* Chewing away at my insides, any opportunity to fuck my self over, I took it. I relished the opportunity to dine on any values I had left that resembled anything meaningful or true. I mourned the loss of myself, even though I had no idea who I was. I wanted to be anyone other than myself.

Maybe you can relate.

You might not believe you've lived a life worthy of a memoir, but you have. We all have. You don't need to write your story down to heal though. You'll see yourself in my story, and you'll find peace and empowerment, like I have. Going back in time can be hell, but it's worth it. Truth is never simple. It almost always comes with chaos and complicated questions. But we'll be going there together, so you won't be alone.

Who are we, really? Can we really change? And how does one make amends when those who've we've hurt us are long gone? Speaking one's truth without being angry or vindictive can be difficult, but it's an important and meaningful way to resolution. Not settling scores or being mean. Simply finding a way to forgive yourself and others when possible and appropriate. In the end, you might find yourself celebrating your past more than regretting it. I do.

No one wants to read a pure "misery memoir," in which the author laments and seeks pity for the many terrible things that have happened to them. This book confronts dark truths, but it's also entertaining. We must speak our truth. Silence equals death for abuse survivors, if not a literal death, certainly an emotional one. And the only option left: betray the abuser.

Keep yourself quiet, like a good boy. Well, I'm not a good boy anymore. Not that type of good boy.

Maybe you can relate.

Chapter 1
Dallas 1989

One day I received a package with a video cassette and a set of Polaroids in the mail from my former high school Drama teacher.

Larry Lane Bateman and I kept in contact over the years. Postcards and the occasional phone call. I held onto the belief he had been a good influence on me when I was a teenager, that he shepherded me out of the gay closet on Long Island, that our interactions had been special but normal nonetheless, even though the world would hardly be able to understand what we did together or more appropriately, what he did to me. He was the adult, after all, me his teenage student.

The content of the first video was quite intense—a mix of adult, teen and kids; vanilla, jocks, twinks, and bondage—highly edited with music and graphics to make the clips appealing, stimulating and in some cases sickening.

But the Polaroids, they really got my attention. The Polaroids were of me when I was Larry Lane Bateman's 16-year-old student. Why did he send them? They were sexually explicit and part of a special "away-from-school" video project he arranged, a project I was supposed to keep secret, and had for over ten years.

My god, who is this boy, I asked? Is he having fun? His eyes seem dazed. I don't remember much, it's all kind of hazy. I was drunk and high, the amyl nitrite had lifted me out of my body, as well as my legs, apparently, which were lodged well above my head. I was totally exposed. Was I proud of this? Why did I do it? To please him. Yes, to please my teacher and stay safe in his arms forever.

I thought he was my friend. He was vested in me believing so. I was vested in it too, because the alternative was impossible to fathom.

7

CAPABLE OF BETRAYAL

Chapter 2
Marianna, Florida 1960's

I was born at the Fort Gordon army base in Augusta, Georgia.

A simple start to a complex life.

After a year, we left and I've never felt the need to go back.

Mom (Maribeth Jo) and father (Phil) had nothing in common other than sexual fireworks in the bedroom.

Maribeth was trying to find herself (or deny her true self), and with Phil she had a way out from her lesbian tendencies and desires. And women, they both loved women.

Soon into their marriage it became clear Phil had intense psychiatric issues, waves of manic behavior where he would speak non-stop for extended periods, with or without an audience. And he would go on drinking binges for days at a time, self-medicating or feeding the mania. And wind up in deep funks and stay isolated in bed.

Maribeth's dad, my grandfather, whom I'd call Grandpomp due to a speech impediment, was a circuit judge in small town Marianna, smack in the middle of the Florida panhandle.

(I called his 2nd wife Granchar as I couldn't pronounce Grandmother Charlotte.)

Well, no surprise, Grandpomp and Granchar launched a campaign for Maribeth Jo and Phil to separate and divorce, in their view for everyone's safety.

Being a high-profile judge in an itty-bitty southern town with its own share of petty crime, civil fraud and dramatic divorce cases, he kept a loaded handgun in the glove compartment of his huge dark blue Lincoln Town Car. I was intrigued by the gun and out of curiosity tried to get to it in the glove compartment. Wisely, it was locked up.

I loved standing on the roof of said Town Car, feeling quite important and fancy in my Easter outfit—colorful bowtie, linen sportscoat and tan pants with brilliant blonde-white crewcut hair.

"Like a Prince," Grandpomp would say.

Long before ancestry.com, regular folk did genealogical studies and Grandpomp's was a doozey. He was convinced we were but 500 people away from the UK crown. A flight of fancy, for sure. (But

9

later on, I'd watch the movie "The Prince and the Pauper" and find myself identifying with the struggles of both prince and pauper. Along with the fantastical lines of having too much money and the freedom that money buys, I'd become keen on Richie Rich comics.)

I also loved going to his Judge's chambers, grabbing the gavel and banging for order on his huge antique paneled oak desk, en route to becoming a vintage piece.

In addition to banging Grandpomp's gavel, I sought the spotlight at an early age. Granchar was a big Johnny Carson fan and she told me that during his opening monologues, he stood on a plastic gold star affixed to the stage. "One day you'll stand on a star, little Mike-o," Granchar would say. "Mike-o" was Granchar's nickname for me.

And I wanted to. *I wanted to be a star.* Granchar's star. Someone people looked up to and applauded. Someone Granchar would be proud of. Someone important.

Marianna was famous for three things: its limestone and flowstones caverns; the boarding school horror at Dozier School for Boys (fictionalized in Colson Whitehead's "The Nickel Boys"); and native Van Smith, who was legendary drag queen Divine's make-up artist. Jim Crow south and lynching but sadly that's part of Marianna's heritage too.

Granchar would travel all the way to Tallahassee for John Waters' Divine movies. She celebrated John Waters with pink plastic flamingos she fabricated for her front lawn on Green Street. "Nobody knows why I do that, except for my *specials*. It's our *secret signal*," she'd say of her ongoing coterie of gay and trans friends she'd make over the years in that little town. Of course, she didn't understand John Waters' movies but loved the characters' eccentricities and Van's make-up for Divine. Van was Granchar's best friend Eloise's son. We were mighty pleased Van would receive an obituary in the *New York Times* after he passed away years later.

The Elks Club in Marianna, one of around 100 lodges from the pan handle to the Keys, private and by-invitation-only, was my introduction to sirloin steaks. I loved 'em rare with their distinctive bloody smell but Granchar only ate the fatty grizzle portions of her steaks, don't know why. Granchar cackled when I'd eat watermelon at Elks Club barbeques, spittin' out them demon seeds while crunching and slurping away. After we'd arrive some nights, I'd sneak off to the auditorium, turn on the mic on a side table and announce, *Here's Johnny!* over and over to the confused crowd dining on steak and imbibing illegal alcohol with the sheriff, my granddaddy the judge and his former law partner-fellow public defender Virgil Quincy Mayo. (Marianna was notoriously dry but not at the Elks Club, which promotes itself as non-partisan and patriotic, promoting the wellbeing of life which to my eyes included lots of folk from the St. Luke's Episcopal Church, big fifths of whiskey and big fuckin' steaks.)

And Virgil Q Mayo, a cross between Winston Churchill and Boss Hogg, was my first experience knowing an alcoholic, and one who openly bragged: "I keep Playboys in all the bathrooms of our home. My boys were raised on Playboy! No fruities in this house!" (All four of his boys got married but two divorced and came out as gay. Virgil was crushed.)

Grandpomp and Granchar would always ensure that whiskey bottles on site were kept at low levels…because when Virgil Quincy Mayo showed up, all bets were off. For a voluminous drinker, though, he laughed a lot and was the center of conversations at the Elks Club and at Grandpomp's ranch style home on Green Street.

And then silence. Virgil stopped drinking. "I'm a drunk, not an alcoholic" he'd say.

From this I learned: No alcohol, no fun.

I missed the old Virgil and his seemingly out of control laughter that took the oxygen out of any room he was in.

My beloved Granchar, well she was my very own Auntie Mame!

We had our secrets because she understood me.

"We were all born bored, Mike-o," she said. "We need some excitement! Keep things interesting."

She knew I was different and liked feminine things. Away from prying eyes, we'd apply clear nail polish to my dainty little fingers because I liked how it all made me feel—putting on nail polish and Granchar's Shalimar perfume were our delicious little secrets. "Who is Queen of this house?" she'd ask. "You are," I'd say. "I'm the Queenie of England! Someday I'm gonna be 'wich!" But soon enough Grandpomp would realize what we were up to. "He'll grow up to be a fruit," Grandpomp bellowed. But Granchar and I didn't care. I'd try on her high heels and skirts. Of course, too big and draped on me. Still, I liked the femininity of these games. Granchar and I would look at me in the bedroom mirror all dragged out in girls clothes she bought at the flea market and giggle to the high heavens. "Such a pretty girl," she'd say. "And I smell so pretty, too!" I gleefully added. I'd eat the gin infused olives in Granchar's afternoon happy hour beverages—and get lightheaded although they tasted awful. One day I got all dressed up, put on some of Granchar's make-up, crossed Green Street, large, scary vines from the ancient-seeming trees hanging down ready to gobble everyone up, and knocked on friend Ronnie's front door. His mom, Helen, the neighborhood gossip, couldn't get on the phone quick enough to call Granchar and tell her what her little *granddaughter* was up to! When she got home, Granchar was stern. "These dress-ups are our fun and not for anyone else!" So we kept our magical fantasia behind closed doors.

I'd try to kiss Grandpomp once, and he pushed me away. "Men don't kiss." I didn't understand but realized that the stubble on his cheeks were pointedly painful, so perhaps that's why and better to avoid anyway. At least that's what I told myself. But even then, I felt shame for expressing my feelings, if just a harmless kiss on my Grandpomp's stubby cheek.

Maribeth Jo had gotten a master's in education from Florida State University (FSU). She was a respected member of the FSU Flying High Circus and with her small body an easy catch on the high wire and a fast tumbler. Over the years, the FSU Circus big top suffered terrible destruction when tornados roared through the state capital Tallahassee. Proudly wearing a Seminole Flying High Circus tank top, Maribeth dated men and women on campus and had a brief affair with FSU football legend Fred Beletnikoff. "Fred was almost your Daddy," she'd say.

Maribeth Jo's first teaching job was in Oklahoma so that's where we headed in a beat-up jalopy, Maribeth free of Phil thanks to a quick divorce. We were dirt poor living in a non-airconditioned perspiration filled house full of strong, tough women, some bikers, all openly bisexual or lesbian.

Maribeth Jo?

Are you kidding?

In that house, mom was known simply as *Jo*.

Grandpomp wasn't crazy about Maribeth's tomboy lesbian-like hairstyles and he and Granchar spoke at length about Maribeth Jo's sexuality. They were hoping she'd grow out of it. Eventually she would but at what cost?

You can run but you can't hide from who you are.

I loved hanging on to *Jo's* girlfriend Ree's back on Ree's souped-up motorcycle. I'd yelp up to the flying angels while Ree would laugh and tell me to *man-up* and not be a *sissy-boy.*

Because everyone knew I was destined to be a sissy-boy.

Sissy-boy.

Running around the house butt-naked on Green Street.

Proud to be letting it all hang out.

Because the world hadn't yet done what it does to idealistic young boys.

Excitedly entering the front porch of my grandparents' Florida Vernacular designed home and presenting a frog I'd found to Granchar. She slammed the door shut. "Mike-o, throw that frog in the garden where it belongs!"

Making a ruckus across the street to Ronnie, who would also become my first male fascination. Throwing the Monopoly set in the air when I lost to Ronnie, game pieces and funny money flying everywhere along with my angry screams.

"I hate this game," I'd yell.

Ronnie and I kissing—with a couch pillow between us—pretend kissing. I'm pretty sure Ronnie was thinking about a girl. I was thinking about Ronnie.

Ronnie intuitively knew I was different, cut from a different personality cloth, not just because I'm from the north but because he probably suspected I loved him deeply. And there was no way—kissing with pillows notwithstanding—he could return my love.

But before focusing on Ronnie, I was quite fascinated with lady parts and boobs and luxe romantic attire via Playboys that my Granchar would furtively buy for me. Away from the eyes of Maribeth Jo (who would disapprove and say that *real men don't need porn*), both Granchar and I were enthralled with the buxom Playboy playmates on the glossy pages. Perhaps not just admiring them, I wanted to *be* them?

CAPABLE OF BETRAYAL

Of course, in Marianna, other than the going's on at the local Greyhound station bathrooms (I was forbidden to play pinball at the Greyhound station...but a pinball lover, I did anyway; I'd watch men go into the restrooms and stay longer than usual. What went on in the bathrooms? Was it fun? Couldn't be, seemed too scary and the eyes of the men looked vacant, I pee-peed at home), there weren't any alternative outlets for Granchar and Grandpomp (years later though Granchar would become a magnet for transgender and queer folk in Marianna via the pink flamingos she curated and kept on the front lawn as a way to draw them to her front porch for conversation, cigs and hooch). In the late '50's, early 60's they'd head to New Orleans for some transgender entertainment, the kinds of characters and personalities not openly found in little Marianna. I don't know what their arrangement was. Grandpomp had numerous health issues, including TB as a teenager and young adult. By the time he was remarried to Granchar, I suspect their bedroom activities were quiet. So, the bohemian culture of the French Quarter and all the strange and weird happenings were catnip for my grandparents. They had a regular drag haunt Club My-O-My and every visit the flamboyant MC Gene La Marr would plant a huge, wet and drowning-in-red lipstick kiss smack on Grandpomp's lips, to his absolute delight! My grandparents returned to Marianna with lots of stories of drag shows, gay bars and same-sex illegal dancing in the clubs. Though most of those stories they kept to themselves.

For my 9th birthday, Ronnie gave me a brand-new cassette tape of Elton John's Greatest Hits album along with a tee shirt with a picture of the album cover. How did Ronnie know to choose Elton John's music as a gift? How did I know, when I looked at the picture of Elton John, that Elton was sending me a message with his confident smile and snazzy all-white outfit? He certainly knew about being himself, something that I longed for...to be fully myself. At that point, I felt out of place with everyone and everywhere, except with Granchar in Marianna.

Biological father Phil showed up once in Marianna, blithering incoherently and wanting to see me—on directions from my grandfather, housekeeper Francis locked us in the bathroom until he left. "Stay here baby. We're safe," she reassured me.

Another time I was riding my bike on Green Street, took a tumble and really tore up my knee with an open gaping wound. A man in a large car pulled over and offered to help me. I remembered what Granchar said about *stranger-danger*. "Mike-o, if any man offers you something or wants to take you somewhere, he up is to no good and probably wants to rape you."

"I don't want to be '*wapped*, Granchar!"

"You just get away, scream if you need to and get home, you hear?" I got on my bike and got as far away from him as I could, snot rolling across my lips and tears running down my little cheeks, grateful not to be '*wapped*, whatever that was.

But we're taught to trust our teacher's, yes? No stranger-danger there, right?

Chapter 3
Dallas 1989

By now I had a closet full of porn that my former teacher had sent me. I should be happy, yes? So much to wank off to, yes? But I was living alone in a small sparsely furnished one-bedroom apartment in Dallas, ostracized from the gay bar empire family I'd been a part of, that I was supposed to be heir to, my father-by-adult adoption pushing weeds in Pennsylvania, gone to the gay bar empire in the sky. Larry Lane Bateman is my friend, isn't he? That's why he sent all this porn? And those Polaroids? They were the pinnacle of our union, when I gave him all of me ten years earlier as a 16-year-old in the hopes we'd live happily ever after. But I'm living in a dream world, nowadays only lamenting what could have been and how awful the present moment is. Back to wanking. Cause my teacher taught me well, how my worth is as a sexual object, right? And despite it all, I can still get the sex right. Despite it all.

Still, I felt an emptiness inside, an abyss that seemingly had no end. A hatred of who I was and what I was doing and how I was living my life, even though I had no fucking idea who I was, how I got here and where I was going.

Chapter 4
Long Island & Queens 1970's

After Oklahoma, Maribeth and I headed to Queens, New York ... an enclave known as Richmond Hill to be exact, off Liberty Avenue, even then a league of nations of sorts, a melting pot of Italian, Irish and soon-to-arrive Indo-Caribbean folk.   Maribeth had landed a job in tony Manhasset public schools on Long Island as a high school history teacher, about a 45-minute drive via the Long Island Expressway, known non-affectionately as the world's longest parking lot. Her first big teaching job. And where she would teach for the next 30 years.

Sorry but I have another grandmother to introduce you to.

Maribeth's Sicilian mother, Muriel Bancie, my Nana. (Bancie's latin roots are: "cool, beautiful, unique" which sums up Nana's 20's although she was a lot more.)

So, in the south was Granchar, really the good witch (if we were to view them as witches) and in the north was Nana, the truly angry witch who had no use for anyone except me, her dog Willie, cat Miriah and men who paid the bills, her days of youthful beauty bitterly long gone.

Nana was a tough broad. Beneath her hair bun—a daily feature—and drawn on eyebrows—also a daily feature—is a woman who navigated abusive men, men who at the time felt they could take what they wanted from women. A woman who had been used and abused by men. (After Nana's passing years later, I found an unsettling picture of her uncle kissing a surprised 10-year-old Nana on the lips and asked Cousin Shirley about it. Shirley just shook her head and looked down.) Muriel eventually beat them with her own rules of the game.

Why give it away when you can get something for it?

A gangster's mole, girlfriend to famous politicians, including former Mayor Jacob Javits (and perhaps even Roy Cohn), amassed a small fortune through patient savings and compound interest, the most profitable bonds at the time and a paid-off her Queens Richmond Hill multi-family Victorian brownstone as a result. Yet, later in life, Nana would languish in her upstairs apartment, and long-time renter in the lower apartment Mrs. Barnes would never invite Nana for holiday dinners with her adult foster children. Nana would lament loneliness in what should be the golden years but vodka and cigs went some way to numb the pain.

Her unit on the 2nd floor, well it was once probably fabulous and in-style in the fifties; but now stark, gloomy, old fashioned; a permanent haze of soot—dusty lamps, tables, lighting fixtures, ratty brocade sofa that was once plush and grand; a long unused upright piano languished along the north wall. And requisite plastic on the lounge chair—for what? Me jumping on it, I guess. The stench of old. And back then as a kid stuff that was old smelled and looked it ten-fold.

"Flipper!"

(Flip is short for my first name Philip—Michael is my middle name-- and when intoxicated--which was often—the best Nana could do was Flip or Flipper.)

"Flipper," wine breath and cigarette smoke cascading down on my little head, "They think they have the power. I showed them all," her words one big, long non-stop slur.

Mom, whom I will call Maribeth frequently in these pages, and I moved into the first-floor apartment in Nana's brownstone after arriving from Oklahoma. I even had my own bedroom, a single bed with utilitarian metal headrest attached to the frame along the wall by the window into the alley. It was always shady and sometimes I saw first floor occupants in the next building. A small orange pumpkins hung by a string on the window shade. I'd stare at the pumpkin for hours on end. The summer heat sweltered. Nana did not believe in air conditioning. "We will not make the electric company rich!" But she certainly owned a lot of ConEdison and other utilities' stocks.

Nana loved me like no one else. I was truly the apple of her eye. She hated adults but loved kids and dogs. Why? *Neither kids or dogs can hurt her.* Atop her refrigerator a piggy bank in the shape of a big jowl Basset Hound with droopy ears; she'd put quarters in and say with a big smile, "One day dahl they'll be yours."

Nana would take me to Coney Island on the subway, and this began my love affair with all things surf, waves, and sandy beaches. We'd walk for hours on the boardwalk; I'd smother my face in a big cotton candy sugar confection (which I adopted its nickname 'fairy floss') and of course a hot dog from Nathans. We also visited Atlantic City, Nana palming the $10 in quarters given by the casino. I loved smelling the sea and running on the beach. But the ocean was off-limits.

Nana would get tickets to television shows: we were in the studio audience for an episode of "Beat the Clock." I coughed in the background hoping I'd be able to hear it when we watched the episode at home. Also *Mame* with Pearl Bailey on Broadway. Both experiences—along with my infatuation with Johnny Carson with Granchar in Florida—added to my infatuation with entertainment and the stage.

Little Willie our Boston Terrier was quite put off when I tried to eat his dinner out of his bowl one night in Nana's upstairs apartment. That led to an emergency room visit to Forest Hills Hospital with me yelping: "Willie bittie me! Willie bittie me!" Mom wanted Willie put down and of course Nana refused. My face swelled up red as a balloon but eventually returned to normal; the little scar from Willie's bite receded over the years.

Across the backyard, above-ground subway tracks shot across the rear of the property, causing our building to shake so hard we'd usually have to stop speaking and wait for the subway car to pass noisily by before continuing the conversation. If there were seatbelts on the kitchen chairs, I would have put them on.

Nana also loved buying me stuff. "Whaddya want, doll?" I told her a paint set. Downstairs in Maribeth's kitchen I was able to paint watercolors and be creative, which seemed like a natural fit. I enjoyed applying colors to shapes, skies, and landscapes. I did a pretty accurate portrait of Woodrow Wilson.

And Nana loved wine. Lots of wine. Her boyfriend Herman "Lemke the Plumber" would say at dinner, "Woman, the more I drink the drunker you get." Herman the German," my nickname for him (although really it should be Herman the Nazi with his perverted version of German history) would take us to a high-end Italian Queens restaurant named Luigi's with the decor of the Vatican.

It was always a scene.

Nana would invariably enter a black-out stage, not sure if dinner had been served (it had) and would argue with what she called *lowly* waitresses.

A band played on Saturdays. While belting out "I Will Survive," the drummer would put up a sign: "Mona Lisa has gas." I'd giggle every time.

Sometimes I'd find Nana passed out nude on her kitchen floor, fluorescent lights shining down on her glistening bare skin. I thought the worst. I'd scream, "Nana, are you alive?" She'd mumble something incomprehensible. "Nana, get up!"

"Doll, I'm at the happy place," she'd finally drawl.

I'd help her to bed, my hands slipping along her sweaty torso, and return to the kitchen and its godawful antiseptic overhead lights.

How can I stop her drinking?

As an eight-year-old, I was already thinking about fixing the adults in my life and their problems.

I figure if Nana doesn't have money, she won't drink. So, I'd go into her purse, pull out all the money from her wallet and put the cash in the trash. Not sure if she ever retrieved the cash but her drinking certainly continued.

Herman would take Nana to the hospital every now and then, usually around midnight. She was intoxicated and incoherent. I slept in the waiting room. I don't know if the 3–4-hour treatments involved replacing her blood or vitamin infusions or tranquilizers for detoxification or what. But Nana would seem steadier a few hours later. And of course she didn't stop drinking.

I'd overhear them panting and grunting in the bedroom. Of course, I didn't understand but I did see Herman nude and partially erect when he went to the bathroom.

I also learned how to lie from Nana and Maribeth.

Mom was teaching on Long Island and didn't want me to attend school in Queens. Mrs. Anderson's Nursery School in Great Neck on Long Island became my "residence" so I could attend a nearby higher quality public school. At one point, the school principal suspected I didn't live at the nursery school. I was called into her office and honestly told her that I lived in at Nana's house and mom dropped me off at Mrs. Anderson's every morning. Later Mrs. Anderson would scream at me, Maribeth would scream at me and slap my face and Nana would yell, "You weren't supposed to tell the principal the truth!"

I felt humiliated and beat up on myself—for telling the truth.

And I'd act out my anger and rage, neither of which I understood nor had the capacity to express in healthy or safe ways, even as a kid. Maribeth's longtime friend Barbara's family lived on Long Island. For Maribeth, Barbara's family was the family she always dreamed of having, and we regularly spent weekends with this family. I'd watch TV in the basement. One time, out of the blue, I took a paper clip, straightened it and carved up the top of one of the coffee tables...circles, triangles, figures of people with unhappy faces. I truly destroyed the beautiful shiny wood top of that table. The look on Barbara's face, the face of her sweet mom Grace, her sisters and of my mother were looks of astonishment, sadness, concern and fear.

I could hear them whispering: Maribeth, your son needs help. Maribeth shook her head. I'll deal with it.

Later back in Queens Maribeth would strap me and slap me. "You are pathetic," she screamed. "How could you embarrass me like that in front of my friends?"

Another way I acted out was biting my nails...down to the quick. Later I'd learn this is a form of self-mutilation, but the act of gnawing gave me comfort and relaxation. Maribeth would put Band-Aids on my bloody fingers, and another thing to yell at me about.

Maribeth purchased a 1967 baby blue Mustang automobile and was proud that she didn't need Nana's support—she'd saved the entire down payment. She also saved enough to put Nana through a 3-day detox from alcohol. Nana declined. "Why would I give up something I enjoy so much?" she asked.

Yes, I'd come to understand this all too well.

During these years Maribeth was beyond strict with me. I was expected to sit at attention all the time and behave perfectly. "Let him be a kid," Nana would say. Maribeth preferred to slap me, either on the buttocks or face if I stepped out of line or was simply being a kid. Maribeth regularly called me *dumb* and *stupid.* For a mother determined not to have a *retard son* she certainly drummed into me how *dumb* I was.

Maribeth was needy. Big needy eyes with dark circles. Like weapons. And I was powerless to not meet her needs, as unfair as that sounds. Being sucked into her vortex of need, a one-way ticket to unbearable sadness and a belief that I'm responsible for all her unhappiness.

She'd come into my bedroom and lay next to me. She'd push herself up against me repeatedly. Me dripping with sweat and fear. If I choose to (I don't), I can still smell her. If she did anything else during what she called "love sessions" I do not recall. Perhaps it's good that I don't. But my brain swirled.

I can't breathe. Why are you on top of me? Pushing. Pressing. Obliterating. Overwhelming my personal space with your smelly perspiring body. Not seeing me as a human being but as your little personal doll.

Are you trying to squeeze the queer out of me?

Are you pushing your privates on me...to cause a desire or interest? Is that how afraid you were I'd be a homosexual?

Soon thereafter I had the most vivid dream of my life. My little body rising up through Nana's Queens brownstone...out of Maribeth's apartment, into the shared hallway, up through Nana's apartment, like an apparition, and my penis...my penis has separated from my body. I'm panicked and flailing, trying to get it back and reattach it.

My entire body is an empty vessel.

I don't want to be in it anymore.

I just want to fly away.

Chapter 5
Queens - Long Island 1970's

Maribeth met a fellow teacher at Manhasset High School.

Initially it was all extremely exciting. I was desperate for a male figure in my life. As an effeminate kid with wild unruly hair, dumbo ears and Buddy Holly glasses, everyone warned Maribeth that I was on my way to being *a fag*. The only solution: a strong male father-figure at home.

Fred taught me how to throw and catch a baseball. He taught me how to shake hands *like a man.*

Fred never let me forget how lucky I was that he was raising another man's son.

That's what I was.

Another man's son.

Maribeth and Fred would marry via a Justice of the Peace in Hempstead, Long Island. Nana attended as did a few close teacher friends. I'd throw rice at Maribeth and Fred like Nana told me too. Maribeth was upset the rice got in her eyes. By then, it seemed I could do nothing right.

But now I have a stepfather.

Maribeth and Fred's plan to *bulldoze the homo out of me* was well underway.

I joined a midget baseball league with Fred as a coach. In addition to baseball, Fred introduced me to lacrosse. Unlike basketball where it helped to be tall (I wasn't) or football where it helped to be big (I wasn't) with lacrosse you can be any size and play. And with strong skillsets, it's possible to excel at this sport. We all noticed that I had a natural talent for managing the lacrosse stick and accurate throwing (I could hit a dime from 20 yards away). I was quick as a whip and had to be to avoid the hits and abuse from defenseman (I played the scoring position...attack).

With lacrosse I became more comfortable with the totally uncomfortable masculine and aggressive player-to-player experiences. I learned about teamwork and cooperation. The paint set Nana gave me had to go; same for my beloved Elton John posters I'd hung in the bedroom of the 1.5-acre Old Brookville home Maribeth and Fred purchased (but could hardly afford). The focus was to *man me up*. In the process I was a placed in a locker room with other naked boys my age. Rather quixotic thinking, I would say. Around 13-years-old my sights shifted from the big boobs of *Playboy* to the jockstraps of my teammates and the all too often homoerotic shenanigans of the showers. The smell of the locker room enthralled me, fascinated me, captivated me. Young men's sweat; the sounds of the water spraying in the showers. Hoots and hollering. Checking each other out. Jockstraps. Butts in jockstraps. I guess that's why guys like thongs on women so much.

One of my teammates once entered the shower area with a slight erection. Lots of laughter and mocking. *Is it your first time, darling?*

And so began my lifelong fear of getting a hard-on in a locker-room. It also meant a visual inspection of my wares and the wares of other boys. I'd be described as a "grow-er, not a show-er." The kiss of death as my dick is pretty small un-erect. Some guys seemingly had dicks down to their knees un-erect. But most were very average. As a grow-er, mine was on the small side and with it a lot of shame and feelings of inadequacy.

Still the locker-room scenes fueled my budding same-sex attractions. One obsession was JJ. This guy was as perfect as they come: gorgeous thick light brown hair, dense sexy eyebrows, luscious lips, Hollywood cheekbones, a smile so sweet yet seductive everyone was taken by it. And a body and bum that did not quit. He loved to sit on top of his desk, tight corduroy pants, legs spread with a perfect view of his crotch. When he showered at the gym, he sensuously spread liquid soap over his fine lithe body, easily a living likeness of Michaelangelo's David. He knew he was his own pleasure island; we were allowed to admire but not touch. JJ was never bullied; he was so cool none of bullies ever dared. He was my junior and high school crush and saw me through early puberty fantasies. I'd fantasize about being his girlfriend as he was frantically losing his virginity. "Yes JJ give it to me, baby!"

On the lacrosse field, I had the opportunity, whether I wanted it or not, to practice courage. In one instance, a coke-machine defenseman on the other team charged me: I could either run to the side or take the hit. I took the hit and was knocked out cold. I came to and looked up to see Maribeth's newly acquired big boobs staring down at me. "Michael, are you okay?" In my delirium I thought it was Dolly Parton had come to my rescue.

"Dolly, is that you?" I asked.

Then Dolly's face changed to Tammy Faye Bakker.

"Tammy! I've been trying to call you at the PTL Club!"

Maribeth and Fred and the coach lifted me up and walked me to the bench, the coach declaring: "Men, that was courage in action. Mike took the hit instead of side-stepping!"

But the coach wasn't always so complementary. At the end of the season at the lacrosse team awards dinner, I was the butt of the coach's remarks, literally and figuratively.

"Everyone, Mike was our top scorer. All the more amazing as he is a lard ass and can barely make it from one end of the field to the other. Amazing that a lard ass could score so many goals. Anything is possible."

There was mixed laughter and applause, all seemed awkward. There was silence in the car home as Maribeth, Fred and I processed what had happened. What would Fred do? Staying calm, he just called the coach and asked why he made jokes at my expense. Coach proffered some excuse about breaking the ice and apologized for the inappropriate remarks. Maribeth and Fred let it go; beside we needed the coach to start me and promote me to university recruiters. Still, it reinforced my negative body image because yes even though I was short and small I was heavy in the seat.

Maribeth and Fred took every unresolved issue in their life to each other in what would become our own "War of the Roses." Going to bed at night, I knew there was the probability of 3am screaming and breaking of furniture. Our pet dog General (a thoroughbred boxer) and I would cower in my bed. The next morning I'd go downstairs to the scene of the most recent destruction: smashed dinner plates, broken chairs, phone taken apart so Maribeth or I couldn't call the police.

I regularly fantasized I'd be adopted by The Brady Bunch. God they were so normal compared to us.

Also, the long reach of the Trump family made its way into our household; it felt as though we were living in their shadow from Manhattan and Trump Tower out on Long Island. This isn't meant to be political; it was just our reality. Fred found Donald (he called him *The Donald*) to be the epitome of manhood and success (along with the character Captain Kirk on the TV show Star Trek and James Bond 007); Maribeth patterned her whole appearance—caked on make-up, thick red lipstick, bright bleach blonde hair in a bun—after Ivana Trump (and a way for Maribeth to hide her true self under all those layers of foundation goop). Although the Trump's lived an extraordinary lifestyle compared to most of us on Long Island, it was out of reach and impractical; yet so many of us aspired to that level of what seemed like greatness, fed by *Page 6* in *The Post* and ongoing splashy news stories of the Trump family and business soap opera. My Nana, who was often the other woman in her younger years, was obsessed with Marla Maples. "Marla this, Marla that, Marla, Marla, Marla" she'd go on, lamenting that Marla got screwed in the end.

My respite from the insanity of our Long Island home life were summer holidays in Florida. For Maribeth and Fred, it gave them the summer to themselves and their crazy. For me, it was a godsend.

Grandpomp had passed away a few years earlier, Maribeth convinced (in part because Granchar did not cry at his funeral) that Granchar had him murdered by the town elders because she was sure of rope burns on his wrists in the coffin.

Granchar had settled in as Marianna's premier Judge's widow.

As a young teenager, my summers in Marianna brought me quiet, peace and some curious awakenings.

When my airplane landed in the Dothan Alabama Airport and taxied to the one gate, I'd open and close the window shade—up and down—because I knew Granchar was watching. My excitement to see Granchar on these trips overflowed with relief and joy.

Granchar would say, "It takes you about a week to shake off Long Island, Mike-o. Now you're a different person."

"Yes I think I'm more myself here," I'd say.

Granchar's essence enveloped me into a sea of calm. I could be okay in my own skin. At least for our summer together.

Granchar maintained an open goal of *spoiling me rotten*. Them her words. And I'd weep like a stolen heirloom en route to the melting pot when it was time to return to Long Island. Granchar regularly spewed invective about the evils of the north. God she hated the north, strange as she was raised in Pennsylvania but never talked about it. In her mind, she was always and forever more a southern lady.

The summer heat in Marianna stammered through you like a fire ball from hell. My love of air conditioning began here. I'd run it at 60' when Granchar was at work. "Mike-o it's like an icebox in here" she'd say. But she didn't adjust it.

I knew every inch of Marianna, having transversed main streets, side streets and back alleys on my souped-up bicycle with shiny metallic back rest that would pass muster and even win an award at any white trash bike show. It's not a big town so it's not a big accomplishment. But I was proud of my knowledge of our little city. Ok city it's not. Hamlet, how's that? Ok, a parking lot known as Main Street and adjacent homes, with all major Christian religions covered in the usual houses of worship, except for Jews and Muslims and Hindi's. They didn't tolerate anything out of the ordinary. In Marianna, we were segregated by religion and race. Look, I'm trying my best here to get you excited for this lost area of the south with plenty of nods to the confederacy. Governor John Milton lays near my Grandpomp at St. Lukes cemetery—having committed suicide rather than face the outcome of the civil war—amidst what seemed like thousand-year-old trees and vines that add to the southern gothic of this place that is stuck in the 1800's or that time forgot, either works. The only restaurants—Jim's Steakhouse and Tony's Italian buffet—offered Marianna's domestic and international fare. That's it. And Wendy's and McD's of course to round things out. Seemed warm and calm to this little stressed kid from Long Island but what the fuck did I know about the horrors at nearby Dozier School for Boys (Granchar would drive us by the school and she'd say "so many bad things happen there" or a history of lynchings in Marianna post-Civil War during Jim Crow?)

It was my summer oasis and I felt at home here with my BFF Ronnie and cannabis sharing BILF Babysitter Lisa, riding my bike past Ronnie's house and mistaking Santa, who was a year-round lookout and forgotten from Christmas on their front porch bench. I'd say "Hey Foster" confusing Santa with Ronnie's daddy. I was undiagnosed near-sighted so never appreciated why Foster didn't say "hey" back. I assumed he was napping. Ordinarily Foster was kind and served as Marianna's tax collector with a laid-back attitude.

"They'll pay when they can." He was eventually voted out of office but had inherited so much land from his mama that it really didn't matter. Ronnie's parents eventually said good-bye to Marianna for Panama City and a scenic beach view, until a hotel went up and blocked said view. Foster and his wife Helen didn't care much, always glued to their stories, a southern euphemism for soap operas. And oh, it was a scandal when a favorite character *fell from grace* and ratings would go through the roof, including inspired bedroom activity. Because inspiration was in small supply in this place of lost angels, Mary and Anna.

Every Saturday afternoon we'd make our way to Dothan, Alabama, in Granchar's green Mercury Cougar to go to the Spa. We'd listen to—and sing to—Don McLean's *American Pie* countless times along with countless farts on my part, me timing them to "Bye-bye." Granchar deserves a sainthood for enduring my teenage squalid gaseous emissions.

Granchar was mighty happy when the new public library in Marianna opened catty-corner to her house on Green Street. She was a voracious reader but on a limited budget. The library opened the world to her.

Granchar had a favorite southern expression when it was thunder storming but the sun was out: *The devil is beating his wife.* When I was younger, housekeeper Francis looked after me. I was a holy terror for Francis, and she me. When it stormed and the devil was doing his thing, Francis would make us get under the big dining room table. During the worst of the thunderstorm and when the clouds were darkest (electricity long gone), she'd close her eyes and begin mumbling in tongues. Her eyes would go back in her eye sockets, the whites of her eyes apparent, and I'd scream and laugh. As Francis was losing her mind and memory, every week I'd give her a can of peanuts to open. And every week she'd forget what happened the week before and open the can and it would explode with a flying beanie. Francis would scream and I'd laugh hysterically. Every week. Poor Francis.

As an outlet, I'd watch the Brady Bunch, The Price is Right (I thought Bob Barker was the perfect man), all the while cutting myself on my hand and arm, small cuts that gave me relief and helped me relax. Of course I kept this activity secret.

I loved going to the Marianna Rocking Roller Rink, just on the edge of town. Owned by Jerry, an Evis lookalike with sideburns around to his chin and large bouffant, and Inez, a before-her-time Elvira, all black with plenty of cleavage and a huge bouffant as well. They were perfectly matched. It was a simple layout: wooden structure for rink and metal railing, popcorn maker and candy stand, couches for chatting and people watching and pinball machines on the perimeter. Strangely, though, instead of framed music group posters, the walls of Marianna Roller Rink were adorned with Jerry's stuffed deer and tiger heads alongside other types of wild game, all seemingly watching us go round and round while frozen in time.

I loved pinball and besides the greyhound station, there were no arcades in town, so I went for the skating and the pinballing. Everyone went wild when Jerry would play ABBA's "Dancing Queen." The final song at the close of every evening: "Don't Leave Me This Way" by Melvin and the Blue Notes.

One Friday evening, Ronnie made out with a girl, Tammy. Well known at the rink for her friendliness toward boys, she was quite assertive with Ronnie, and eventually, in Granchar's living room with me. Granchar came out from her bedroom in a huff and broke us up. I'd never had a tongue in my mouth before, but Tammy was determined to land hers in mine. If Granchar hadn't broken us up that night, who knows how my sexual template would have been altered by a sexual experience with Tammy? From Granchar's perspective we dodged the baby bullet. But what if I liked it? Would that have dissuaded me from boys? I would spend many years wondering if I was a closet or latent heterosexual. Back then, everything seemed so black and white, you're either something or you're not, no in-between, so it was hard to see sexuality in its various shades and possibilities.

CAPABLE OF BETRAYAL

Chapter 6
Bangkok 2017

Prior to leaving Southeast Asia for Peru I laid over in Bangkok with the primary purpose of…getting laid. But not in the usual way. Throughout my adulthood I've always wondered in the back of my mind—am I a closet heterosexual? How might life be different if Tammy and I had gone all the way after our date at the Marianna Roller Rink when I was thirteen years old?

Would that have altered my sexual template?

I'd had experiences with women over the years but usually clouded with alcohol or drugs, and never full intercourse. In the States I'd explored possibly working with a "sacred intimate" but it didn't play out. (Sacred intimates are men and women who work with survivors of sexual trauma and help them heal via intimate sexual experiences.)

If I was going to jump off this bridge, Bangkok would probably be the best bet.

I approached a well established and government-run Soapy Suds venue in Bangkok. The place resembled a 1970`a dark disco…blacks, greys and whites, shiny surfaces…on the ground floor, behind glass, the workers, wearing numbers, showed their wares and personalities to potential customers.

I asked the mamasan if they offered sacred intimate service.

"SACRED WHAT?" she asked.

Before I could respond she pulled out her phone and googled it.

"Oh virgin. You want virgin? Yes we offer virgin role-play!"

I responded it wasn't a role-play or fetish but a real situation.

"I'm the virgin," I insisted.

"Whatever honey. You virgin, OK! We have experienced girl for you."

I was matched with a sex worker who had a nice smile and was very patient.

I had taken cialis and took a deep breath and, as in the past when in uncomfortable sexual situations, closed my eyes and hoped for the best.

The nice thing about a soapy suds venue is that it is relaxing and calm. My sex worker could tell I was struggling but eventually I got there. It was a pleasant experience. I found her breasts to be soft and mushy. I'm still not sure what to do with them. Kiss? Caress? Suck? Dunno. But the experience—it was a sexual act—although enjoyable didn't change my life or awaken the hetero within (in fact, there is no hetero within). I'm glad I did it but came to see I don't need or want to repeat it.

A sexual act does not define one's sexuality. But it can make things interesting. Or at least put to rest doubts and uncertainties.

Chapter 7
Marianna, Florida 1970's

With Granchar working for a local doctor as the office manager and after Francis's passing, I needed to be looked after. Lisa, a local Marianna native, would be my babysitter and at 18 was quite interesting to me. The term BILF did not exist then (*Babysitter I'd Like To Fuck*) but there was stimulating energy between us. Lisa gave me a big gift: experiencing cannabis on Granchar's enclosed front porch. The 14th summer of my life, this discovery led to a thirty-pound weight gain! I'd gotten contact lenses and my parents had paid for plastic surgery to rein in my humungous ears. When I returned to Long Island, I looked completely different and at North Shore High School many of my classmates didn't recognize me. Making my transformation even more dramatic, my parents had purchased elevator shoes, casual and dress-up. Another reason for feeling inadequate. In Maribeth and Fred's view, you needed to be *tall to be successful.*

The transformation was like mousy Clark Kent to super fabulous Superman.

For so long I'd felt inadequate. Big ears. Small showing dick. Long hair (to cover the big ears). Thick eyeglasses. Skinny body and short height. Effeminate. People often couldn't tell if I was a boy or girl. Honestly at times I wasn't sure of my gender.

I returned to Long Island a New Modern Young Man; I'd "turned hot" in the spirit of memoirist Jenny Han's classic quote: "The summer I turned pretty."

Yet the feelings of inadequacy never left. Everything was a band-aid. The new handsome me was icing on the cake. The cake, however, remained hollow, a needy bottomless pit begging for the kind love which seemingly was out of reach. Although we didn't have sex, Lisa my babysitter was certainly sexual toward me, sitting with her legs spread so I could see her panties and pubic hair beneath her ragged jean shorts. I'm sure I was sitting there apparent excitement observing what Lisa was dishing out. I suppose she was waiting for me to make the first move. I hadn't even had an orgasm yet so I really didn't know what to do with my manliness. Besides, my curiosity was rapidly shifting toward Ronnie, other boys and locker-rooms.

When the day came of my first orgasm, I was sitting on the toilet in Maribeth's bathroom. (My parents and I had a code word for when I was having a number two— "I'm having an emergency" so they'd know I was in the bathroom.) Anyhow, I'm reading one of Maribeth's Penthouse Diary magazines (I guess porn that's in literature form doesn't count) and out of nowhere I climaxed. I thought I was having a heart attack and panicked. I ran to Maribeth's dressing room to tell her. She looked awkward and uncomfortable as I shared about the squirting liquid from my penis. "You should talk to your father," she said. Fred was proud of me and said: "You have a lot of pussy in your future, kid!"

Summers in Marianna included attending Sunday services at St Luke's Episcopal Church. St Luke's, in traditional gothic revival style and deeply colored stained-glass windows on Lafayette Avenue, founded in the early 1920's, is known euphemistically as *Live and Let Live Catholic Light.* One Sunday, I sang a solo version of "Onward, Christian Soldiers" in front of the entire congregation, my voice a practical soprano; one of Granchar's confirmed bachelor friends called and gushed how beautiful my voice was, while Granchar rolled her eyes and thanked him.) With their version of watered-down Catholicism, Episcopalians are an easy bunch, the ongoing joke, where there's four Episcopalians, there's a fifth nearby. The church secretary had a robust figure, and all of them I noticed over the years did—is that an Episcopalian and Roller Rink thing? At Vacation Bible School, I loved being with other kids my age and the bible seemed interesting if remote. I remembered Grandpomp's funeral at St Luke's. I didn't understand what was happening other than Grandpomp had gone to heaven, wherever that was.

Frequently at Vacation Bible School I'd get very enthusiastic, run around and cause all manner of disturbance. The beginnings of my Bipolar Express. The rector called Granchar on the phone about my conduct. When she heard the tenor of his message, she hung up the phone on him. As a Southern Lady is wont to do.

Back in Queens, I'd spent part of one summer at camp. One of the counselors exposed himself to me "Do you want to do something?" I shook my head; God I hope he didn't do anything else.

Teachers wanted to hold me back a year as I was struggling in middle school; they felt slowing down would do me good. But Maribeth wouldn't hear of it. "How dare they say you are a retard! No son of mine is a retard."

If you had listened and kept me back a year, that man wouldn't have been able to do what he did. But heart breaking-ly you had to run the show, Maribeth.

Chapter 8
Queens - Long Island 1970's

Long Island.

Where hope goes to die.

Land of Long Island Lolita Amy Fisher and Joey Buttafuoco (yes that's his name).

Long Island: The Florida of the east coast.

The Long Island Expressway, the world's longest parking lot.

There aren't enough negative adjectives to describe the suburban horror known as Long Island.

That being said, there are gorgeous parts of Long Island: Sea Cliff, Old Westbury Gardens, the East Egg (old money) and West Egg (new money) of "The Great Gatsby," Fire Island and the Hamptons.

Maribeth had big plans for me: NY State House Representative, senator, even president; Ivy League education. Lofty goals, totally bonkers and out of reach.

We lived under a cloud of financial distress, Fred and Maribeth always beyond their means, not one, not two, but three mortgages on their new Long Island home (with a carpeted kitchen, something I'd never seen before), the third mortgage a private loan from singer Perry Como's sister, who was a resident in nearby Sea Cliff. Fred and Maribeth were so overleveraged that only an insurance fraud could bail us out.

It did.

My mania would rear its head at our new home. When my parents were out at night, I'd play Beethoven at full volume in our large living room with picture frame windows, and pretend I was conducting the entire orchestra, hopped up on the cheap red wine in the liquor cabinet.

I guarded my mania and manic episodes so well I hardly knew it when I was experiencing them. I just tried to connect the mania to energy and enthusiasm. But it was easy for the onlooker to see that my reactions at times were more than just positivity and regular excitement.

And to General, our boxer.

Poor General understandably had anxiety in our household and would chew on the furniture. But General's nervous acting-out, including repeated attempts to run away (who'd blame him?) meant beatings or strappings from Fred.

One time, after General really went to town on the furniture, Fred shot him up in the garage with a BB gun and pellet rifle, the pellets and BBs lodged in General legs and buttocks for the rest of his life.

"You're a sawed off pollack," Fred would yell at me during one his rages.

Did he mean my height or my dick size? Either or both, I guess.

But I suppose I have forgiven them. I certainly got my revenge years later when their charade was publicly exposed for the fraud it was.

On the upside, I was raised in a household where education was highly valued, and that value stayed with me through an undergraduate degree, master's and associate real estate broker credentials years later.

Still how do I reconcile my parents viewpoint that money is the key to happiness? Stepfather Fred's favorite expression from The Godfather: "Behind every great fortune is a crime."

"Kid, marry into a wealthy family," he'd say, as though that would solve every problem and create a way for me to live easy and happy.

Even so, I was mighty proud of the first $20 I made helping to paint the exterior of our Long Island home. I stood in front of the mirror with the twenty-dollar bill, posing, happy and proud. These twenty-dollar bills would be my ticket to happiness and the beach and ocean I longed for.

Even though I was surrounded by dishonesty, I still aspired to tell the truth, that there was truth out there. I was convinced Jimmy Carter always told the truth and crushed when I learned he didn't. "All president's lie," Fred said. And so began my trip down Cynical Lane, a sad, lonely street with an inner battle at play, a civil war between right and wrong, honesty and dishonesty.

Our family wasn't the only crazy, unhappy one in Old Brookville. Next door, one of Calvin Klein's up and coming executives would regularly call his wife a "bitch" and "cunt" and we'd hear doors slamming. Fred made fun of him for working from 6am to 9pm, trudging back and forth to the nearby Long Island Railroad station to get to Manhattan or back. I think the executive owns an island and airplane or two, by now.

Fred taught me how to fight bullies (and I was bullied mercilessly in the neighborhood and in school, the names the bullies called me were Monkey Ears and Dumbo, and later Trans). He taught me how to play baseball and lacrosse, with the latter I became a star player as a high school sophomore but it was downhill from there.

So, looking back I'm grateful for those things, including the cosmetic surgery to rein in my wildly humungous ears.

Chapter 9
Long Island 1979

I began chatting with my English teacher "Doc Bateman" (as he was known by adoring students at North Shore High School) when he had hall duty.

One of our lacrosse assistant coaches was a student of Dr Bateman at a previous institution years earlier. At that school, he was known as "Master Bateman." The coach said that his nickname from the students at the time: Master-Bation instead of Master Bateman.

Prescient, I suppose. But I was too young to make any connection.

Doc Bateman asked about my home life and seemed to care. In Speech class he gave me high marks and many written complements on assessments. The way he looked at me, his obvious concern, he was someone I felt I could share stuff with and I trusted him. I felt like he understood me. Like my Granchar, he got me.

I had also gotten involved in his high school theatre program, the Viking Masquers. Everyone would agree, Doc Bateman was an amazing teacher and was dedicated to his craft as a drama coach.

One day he suggested an away-from-school project at his house.

I was so flattered.

Me?

A special project?

Yes, I felt special.

"But keep it between us," he said. "Don't want anyone to think I'm playing favs.

I was thrilled!

The project was a video project.

The subject: me.

The scenario the teacher outlined:

"You've just shared a deep dark secret with a classmate friend. You like boys. He is threatening to tell your secret. You are facing exposure in school. You've returned home in shame and decide to commit suicide by slitting your wrists in the bathroom tub."

This is actually what an adult proposed to a 16-year-old needy, vulnerable male student in his private home away from school.

After close-ups of my face expressing fear and anxiety at what would happen when exposed at school, he said the next step is for me to sit naked in his bathroom tub. I did what he said and got naked and sat in his bathtub. He put tea leaves on my wrists and when dropped into water they looked like blood.

Why couldn't I have told him to fuck off? "You trying to get me out of my clothes, creep? You're not my friend or mentor. You're a fucking predator." But alas I didn't have the ability to protect myself and see what this selfish man was doing. And he was smooth, baby. This wasn't his first trip to the rodeo. He knew how to push all my buttons. This was not a level playing field.

Our Doc Bateman videotaped the whole thing.

Later he gave me wine and marijuana. He showed me pornography of male teenagers my own age having sex. The combination of alcohol, cannabis and porn was overwhelming. I was intrigued by the images I saw. It was as though my middle school locker-room had come to life, become an orgy, and every fantasy I could have imagined was being realized on the movie screen he had up in his bedroom.

He said that if anyone from the outside saw this, they wouldn't approve. To continue our relationship, I'd have to keep quiet and also give myself over sexually, or he would end it.

I wanted to please him.

I didn't want to lose this special relationship. He understood me in ways no one else did.

Polaroids were next.

"Get strong for the camera."

I looked at the porn and did.

"Put your legs up in air," he said. "Let's see that beautiful backside of yours."

More porn, weed and poppers.

I was defenseless and swept away.

He kissed me and I kissed back.

For Bateman, the whole thing seemed a production: lighting on a dimmer; music that varied from Dolly Parton (Here you come again) and Bee Gee's (Staying Alive), all "great music to fuck by," my teacher would later explain.

Again, I was defenseless and swept away.

He put poppers (amyl nitrite) under my nose, I became dizzy from the powerful fumes and felt myself lifting out of my body.

Because of the weed, alcohol, and poppers I didn't feel any pain. But I did feel out of control.

Although I was stimulated mentally and deep into the fantasy of the porn on the screen, nothing that he did to me physically aroused me; I did not get erect throughout, except for the Polaroids when I got erect myself with his porn.

There are parts of it that were pleasurable, folks. And that's the biggest cudgel for survivors of sex abuse—acknowledging that some of it was enjoyable while at the same time we know how outrageous the whole scenario was.

Chapter 10
Long Island 1970's

Although the "love" sessions from Queens had long ended and Maribeth's strictness shifted to a "best mate" approach (most times, when it served her purposes), Maribeth would show herself to me (and Fred) continually and in different ways throughout my teenage years on Long Island: sitting on the couch provocatively; walking around the house with barely any clothes on; bending over purposely with everything in the air; throwing her southern region in our faces anytime she could fathom a clumsy excuse to do so.

At some point, my desire to please Maribeth became paramount and part of our sad dance. First thing in the morning, I'd wake up, make Maribeth's coffee, put it in her dressing room alongside fresh iced water; I graded her papers from school. I'd run errands at the nearby convenience store. Fred chided my mother: "It's like he's your in-house personal servant. You're emasculating him, Maribeth!" But the dance continued, as did my people-pleasing, a lifelong habit that never served me well. (A few years later, as an adult, I even told a guy I was dating on Long Island that I had cancer because I couldn't bear to tell him: "No, I don't want to see you anymore.")

Over a decade later in a New Hampshire courtroom, a prosecutor would lament: "Michael is a people-pleaser. Always the answer is yes. Perhaps he'll never overcome it."

One more thing. Or two large things. Seemingly overnight, around when I was twelve, Mom's figure changed dramatically a la Dolly Parton.

I didn't know what happened or how it happened!

. People would point at Maribeth's big new breasts and I felt so much shame and embarrassment.

Where did the new boobs come from?

And...porn...porn played a role in both Maribeth and Fred's lives. They'd argue over Fred's collection while at the same time Maribeth had her collection of Playboys and Playgirls hidden away in her closet with a handy vibrator.

So much in that closet.

And I used the vibrator and the mags. At that point I was most interested in Maribeth's Playgirl magazines. The guy's cocks and bodies were so well defined. One model, a member of a circus: I'd stare at his cock for hours, just mesmerized by its shape and size and beauty. His butt was lovely too.

With Maribeth's Playgirl magazines, I truly began to appreciate the landscape of the intoxicating male form. It filled my senses with awe and a carnality that felt nothing less than a volcano erupting inside.

I also recall Maribeth telling me that Fred told her that after returning from Vietnam, he'd been to see "The Boys in the Band", a movie about gay male culture at the time. She said he said, "I could never live like that."
Why was he even wondering? Was he bi-curious?

Based on his recollections, certainly Fred had some kind of inappropriate relationship with his grandfather as a kid. Maribeth strongly felt something happened between them.

So, his sexual attractions were conflicted. But of course, he would never acknowledge it.

The heartbreak of my narcissistic parents is they could not or would not admit the traumas they inflicted. Instead, they threw crumbs later on and expected gratitude and a forgetting of the past.

How wrong they would be to think that I would dance that dance with them.

Chapter 11
Long Island 1979

"I have to break off our relationship," the teacher said on the phone a few weeks later. By then we had met a few more times, once at his home and trysts in the dark school auditorium during breaks from class sessions.

I was devastated with the news.

I wanted to wake up with Lane Bateman. Have a life with Lane Bateman. "Call me Lane," he'd said. I was besotted, despite the age difference and so on. Yes the sex wasn't so great except for the porn, pot and poppers. But I loved the attention he gave me. I felt special. I felt loved. I felt like I was finding myself, my young gay self.

He encouraged me to meet other students my own age.

Because he'd gotten what he wanted out of me.

Now he's done.

You're soiled goods.

Time to move on.

Doc Bateman suggested I hang out with an adult friend of his. The friend took me to New York City. One of Bateman's plays about older male teacher's seducing younger male students (the play was part of his dissertation, ignored or unread when he was hired at North Shore High School) was running off, off Broadway. We also visited Christopher Street and Greenwich Village. Had dinner at a well-known gay restaurant called Ty's and I saw, with my own eyes, gay couples of all varieties and types seemingly having fun, being happy without fear of judgement or name-calling. It felt wonderful to know I was not alone. There were other gays, couples, people of all ages and sizes, comfortable in their own skin and sexuality. It was a revelatory social experience for this Long Island teenager.

I was drinking Whiskey Sours, which most of the bartenders in the bars we visited—Ramrod, Uncle Charlies, Badlands--laughed at. I got drunk. As the night progressed, I wanted to see more and do more. My chaperone was getting nervous. We'd missed the last train to Long Island and got a hotel room. I called Maribeth to check in.

"Where the fuck are you?" she pressed.

And continued to press.

And Maribeth knew how to press and get info out of me.

Eventually I relented and told her.

"I'm gay. I'm in NYC with a friend. It's great! I'm so happy. Please share my happiness!"

The friend overheard this and was quietly crying in the bathroom. I'd just come out to my mom, after all. Broke the biggest rule in Lane Bateman's world—telling the truth.

The next morning when I returned to the house on Long Island, Maribeth was in bed. I entered her bedroom, leaned over to give her a kiss on the cheek and she sat up, all Linda Blair a la The Exorcist, with deep red blood hatred propelling out of her eyes, and smacked my face.

Hard.

I was surprised, then stunned by Maribeth's rage, her ability to go from best mate "you can tell me anything" to brutal interrogator: "You fucking cornballer. Which are you? The cornballer or the cornballed?"

Before I could respond, she smacked me again. I backed up and slid down the bedroom wall and sat on the floor. I was in shock. Tears flowed. The welt on my face looked like a sideways outline of Long Island. I had to maneuver quickly so this didn't escalate to a major scene with Fred. And god Fred cannot find out about this. So, I did what she and Nana and Mrs. Anderson the nursery school owner taught me.

"Oh mom," I said. "I was drinking. I made it all up. I was with lacrosse buddies last night. We were drinking and clowning around."

She turned to the side, wanting to believe me I'm sure, but knowing deep down that my call from Manhattan a few hours earlier really was truthful.

We didn't speak for a week after that. Nothing was mentioned to Fred. But from then on, we were going through the paces. I needed to get the fuck out of there.

CAPABLE OF BETRAYAL

Chapter 12
Long Island 1970's

Other than Maribeth's ballet lessons ("Your mutha's ballet slippers are the only thing I want to remember about her...she was my little ballerina star," Nana would bitterly say years later.) Maribeth and Nana truly hated each other. They put up with each other because of me. Nana trusted no one except kids and dogs. I was the only human she trusted, as noted earlier, because I couldn't hurt her. Yet.

Nana certainly had to have been disappointed when she learned her baby was a girl. She loathed women in general and saw them as *competition.* A younger, more beautiful version of herself? Unacceptable, for sure. In fact, my grandfather didn't let nana out of his sight through the entire pregnancy, afraid of what Muriel would do if left to her own devices. (And nana never forgave Maribeth the negative impact pregnancy had on her body. Nana's body was her currency, after all.)

Mom on the other hand had to been disappointed she wasn't born a man. Her looks as a young adult veered from butch dyke to total Marilyn Monroe fem. She too resented men.

Regularly, Maribeth and Fred would drop me off to Nana in Richmond Hills Queens for the weekend. They'd see a Broadway show and have down time from me.

I loved spending time with Nana as she always had gifts for me along with a big wet alcohol and cigarette infused kiss. Fred would remark that my attitude was different after a weekend with Nana. That I'd lie and become nasty, just like Nana. I don't recall but I imagine he was spot on.

I do remember one time when Maribeth drove me to Queens for another weekend drop off. Perhaps Maribeth was late or Muriel was too drunk but they laid into each other with an unusual, even for them, ferocity of screams and punches and pulling—and me in the middle, screaming as well, begging them to stop.

And then it came out.

"While I was giving birth at the hospital, you and Michael's father were fucking!"

Nana pulled with all her might to get away from Maribeth, then she glared and growled:

"He wanted me more than he wanted you," she spat. "He wanted a woman, not some stupid dyke girl!"

Nana spat again.

Maribeth began smashing her mother's face.

The Big Reveal.

They are doomed.

It was so loud that neighbors called the police. Nana's pinky finger was permanently mangled from their punching and yanking.

And I wouldn't see my nana again for at least 10 years.

Nana would have her boyfriend Herman the German bring her to our house on Long Island. Maribeth and Fred would hear them pulling up, close the curtains, turn off the lights and tell me not to utter a word. Nana would plead to Fred and Maribeth through the door to allow her to see me. She'd leave gifts on the porch. I wept quietly. After she left, Fred threw out the presents and we pretended like it never happened and everything was ok.

At this point I seethed hatred and rage at Maribeth for cutting me off from my nana. I felt helpless and powerless as nana did. These days if grandparents are cut off, they can pursue legal remedies for access to their grandchildren. Back then that was unthinkable.

Chapter 13

Long Island 1970's

A few years later, with a sophomore lacrosse season that was stellar, my name was frequently in the Long Island newspaper Newsday with the number of goals I scored. Great press got me lots of attention at home. At school too. And made me feel full and successful, temporarily and euphorically, but full, nonetheless.

My earlier experiences with media was my picture on the front page of the small Marianna Florida newspaper for helping the library move; picture in local Long Island press for meeting with local officials as part of a student group from school. I just knew that my name in the paper was good and got me attention.

I craved attention.

Press clippings filled up the emptiness inside.

For a while.

But I needed more.

Much more.

The sophomore prom was fun. My date, Selma, well no one else would ask her out. Her reputation was loose to say the least and she'd serviced most of the football team. But none of those guys wanted to be seen in public with her. Or at the prom. So, we were stuck with each other. Taller and bigger than me, with tremendous cleavage that shook and jiggled in earthshattering ways, we danced like the odd couple we were, and everyone laughed and joked that I was so short and her boobs were so big that when we danced it seemed like her boobs might just drill me into the middle of the earth.

Despite my lacrosse success, things were breaking down at home.

"We'll have no unpleasantness," Maribeth would say, then they'd proceed to try to kill each other.

Their ability to inflict emotional and physical pain on each other was extraordinary—Fred beat Maribeth, facial and bodily bruises; Maribeth would destroy his diplomas, framed photos and medals from Vietnam.

And I was in the middle. Alongside General.

CAPABLE OF BETRAYAL

I would broker their cease-fires. I was their marriage counselor, carrying messages, beseeching them to find common ground. I was petrified they'd divorce and I'd lose my stepfather. Yet at the same time I fantasized that they would divorce, or better yet that I could find some isolated beach, ocean and mountains, where I'd be left the fuck alone.

When it got really bad and Fred was drunk and out of control with beating walls, smashing bottles and kicking cans against the wall in the garage to vent his rage, Maribeth and I would take his credit card and go to a nearby high-end hotel, charge up the card and have a few nights of peace. In the hotel bed Maribeth insisted on spooning me. I was 14 years old. She was hurting so badly; how could I turn her down? Within a week Fred would show up at the hotel restaurant and beg forgiveness and for us to return home. He promised never to yell or rage or hit us or break things. He never kept that promise. So, in future escapes when he'd show up, we'd just shake our heads and call him a liar. But we always went home eventually.

Michael in the middle of their madness and unresolved issues, with poor boxer General by my side. General was my only friend. But he wanted to get the fuck out, too.

Chapter 14
Long Island 1980

I took Doc Bateman's advice and did try to connect with some classmates. I had a BFF who I shared a lot of secrets with (she disclosed once that she encourages her boyfriends to ejaculate on her face so she can rub it in the "ultimate" moisturizer). We'd try to identify any bi-curious guys in our class that I might approach.

A year before Bateman, a close classmate friend had taken my hand when I was over at his house. To this day I regret pushing it away and I don't know why I did. A few months later I would hit his head for no apparent reason. I was wearing a cast at the time and he might have been concussed from the smack. Like many, I had internalized homophobia and I think his overture at the time was a bridge too far.

A lacrosse teammate who would go on to ride the bench for four years at one of the best NCAA lacrosse programs made crude overtures.

He'd turn to me, bend over, spread his butt cheeks and yell, "Fuck my ass, Mike!" in front of God and the world. He was our goalie and had his own special brand of crazy (goalie's usually do) so I wasn't sure if he was kidding or serious. He did seem to enjoy exposing himself, his dick and buttocks to me. I kind of regret not pursuing that as well.

I did hook up with an effeminate student a year ahead of me. We awkwardly attempted oral sex but we weren't really a good fit.

Of course, I missed being with Lane. I missed the life my young naïve self-imagined and was hoping we'd build, even though it was impossible. But I was a vulnerable kid so of course I'm going to be needy for attention—from most anyone.

How dare you put a vulnerable teenager in an emotionally charged situation much bigger than any teen should deal with!

Lane Bateman was laid off and left North Shore High School at the beginning of my senior year and went on to teach at an exclusive prep school on the east coast, Phillips Exeter Academy.

We kept in limited touch. I thought he was my friend.

Years later a prosecutor would say, "We don't know what Michael's future would have been without Mr. Bateman's influence.

CAPABLE OF BETRAYAL

We do know the teacher without conscience helped Michael along his path of self-destruction."

* * *

With the help of Barry, an African American pal and former Alvin Alley dancer, I soon discovered Manhattan's gay nightlife and especially bars on the East Side of Manhattan catering to younger men and their older admirers. Barry knew I was ambitious and showed me where I could show my wares.

The notorious hustler bars. I presented myself to be discovered.

I loved being adored. Wanted. Needed. Lusted after. Coveted. Desired. A strutting little god making my way through a place of enthusiastic fans, tongues, and cocks wagging. Wanting me.

Oh yes, I was with my fans and I ate up the attention.

I loved the dinners and clothes.

I frequently struck up conversations with admirers at the smartly designed with kind lighting Rounds at 303 East 53rd Street (according to operator Charles Scaglione Sr. in his memoir *Camelot Lost* over the years Rounds was patronized by Tennessee Williams, Truman Capote, Andy Warhol and Vladimir Horowitz and was known as *the store* and purposefully built on the surrounding *vibe* of hustlers and Johns in *the loop* making transactions on nearby street corners) or the nearby somewhat more subdued piano bar The Townhouse, higher-end cruising and showing off, under the guise of show tunes. (I never made it to the West forties Haymarket, gritty trade boys and older men looking for value.) I was always hungry and inevitably suggested dinner when meeting someone new, his treat of course. If he didn't measure up, I'd stand up and say, "Thanks for dinner, bye."

I guess you could say I was, among other things, a dinner whore.

James Tillis, a well-known East Side queen who admits he gave up sex because "life is less complicated that way," once told me with excitement: "Young man, oh you have so much fucking ahead of you! A lifetime of screwing your head off; I'd switch places with you in a minute."

Cocaine, like alcohol, was never moderate or recreational for me. I loved planning and prepping for blow (jargon for cocaine), how cocaine made me feel initially—on top of the world, the greatest of the great, invincible, mind racing in vibrant grandiose light. The

52

adrenaline one would feel before jumping off a cliff, *with or without a parachute.*

And then inevitably the crash would arrive. Panic and fear. Quaaludes helped the descent as did weed and more alcohol. But still it was miserable.

All that pain for 15 minutes of brilliance and hours of chasing the dragon. From minute 16 on, the run would continue until all the blow was gone, until eight, ten or 12 hours passed. And misery waited at the end, ready to scoop me up and remind me: *If you were richer, you'd have more blow. More blow and you won't crash. You'll never have to come down.*

Misery aside, I loved the blow of Manhattan, quite often the potent Bolivian fare. If you had blow, I was your friend and I would easily give myself over for a few hours of partying.

So, I guess you can say I was a coke whore.

Indeed, I was.

I became a regular at the infamous after-hours club Crisco Disco in the Meatpacking District, chased Peter Frampton around, partied with Rick James of *Super Freak* fame and met all kinds of characters from legendary drag stars to mafia figures, fellow hustlers, socialites, club kids, and some scary looking motherfuckers. The DJ booth was circular shaped like a huge old-time Crisco shortening can. I was always admitted past the velvet rope at the Crisco Disco 2nd floor VIP room where coke flowed freely as well as other exotic powders offered by owner Hank, who reputedly landed his lover in cement a few years earlier.

The ultra velvet clad chic VIP room at Crisco Disco had a pecking order for couches. The higher-up you were (rich, famous, infamous) the better chance you'd get a couch or comfortable chair. Usually, I'd be able to land a seat somewhere or with a group of interesting people. Or I'd just sit at the bar and try to attract someone fabulous for a chat or a snort. (When I'd return a few years later as Dallas gay bar royalty, me and my entourage had an entire couch that was vacated just for us.)

I asked Barry, my Alvin Alley dancer pal, about the legality (or lack thereof) of Crisco Disco. "Everyone knows, even the Mayor; everyone who needs to get paid off is paid off."

CAPABLE OF BETRAYAL

I made my way to Studio 54 when it reopened after having been closed due to tax evasion. I'd read about Studio 54 on *Page 6* in The *New York Post*, an oasis of celebrity and cool, and I wanted in on the action!

Initially I waited for hours at the velvet ropes, a few nights in a row, until finally Mark Benecke the front door boss let me in.

And did so regularly from then on.

I arrived one balmy night with my date Beth after our senior prom. Masses of people on the Studio 54 sidewalk but Mark saw me and signaled for the rope to be pulled back, a dramatic parting of the waves as we made our way past the gaping onlookers.

Beth breathlessly remarking afterward, "That's the most exciting thing that ever happened to me!"

At 54, all of us in the know called it 54, I met Andy Warhol and was in the background when Ryan O'Neal and Farrah Fawcett were guests (god her hair really was gorgeous).

I went to 54's Gay Night's on Sundays and marveled at seeing and being a part of so many gay men in one place. It was thrilling to take in what seemed like thousands of hot guys dancing, gyrating and sweating on the dance floor to what is now known as trash disco.

I had many mixed feelings about playing lacrosse in high school. Macho physical engagement on the field, the shenanigans of the locker-room, totally uncomfortable in the gear and perspiration of practices and games. The entire production went against my very being as a sensitive creative kid. But I did learn about teamwork and coordination, the joy of making assists so teammates could get the glory and score goals. Those moments made me happy. On the school bus to away-games, we'd sing Blondie's "The Tide is High" in unison. At times, petty rivalries aside, we became one organism, one moveable being, knowing where on the field Andy, Jon or Jimmy would be, and passing the ball just in time to reach their sticks. We were stars of the lacrosse field and there were enthralling moments as the league underdogs. And I'd drive around late at night—drunk--and visit the lacrosse fields I played on, reliving the goals, hits, plays; remembering the tournament in Hampton Sydney prep school in Virginia when I scored a hat trick (and the winning goal in the last 30 seconds) and was carried off the field by my victorious teammates, all of us—including me--still high from the potent hash brownies we'd consumed the night before in the Hampton Sydney dorm; and me emotionally high after spending the previous night in the dorm bunk bed staring into the eyes of ginger-boy Peter, our eyes dancing a dance, neither one of us courageous enough to make the first move.

But nothing could ease the sting of being rejected by every Ivy League school I applied to. Andy was going to Yale; John to Johns Hopkins, Jimmy to Brown. Me—Farmingdale State College on Long Island for a semester, Nana paying its tuition.

It wasn't all Fred and Maribeth's fault. And when I was able, I began to exact my revenge. Acting out with dishonesty about where I was going (gay bars in NYC), who I was dating (Celeste, an *older widow*—Maribeth and Fred ate that up). Misspending household funds on alcohol. Stealing their alcohol. Being truant from school. Smashing up Maribeth's beloved mustang auto that she'd saved for years earlier in Oklahoma. Using their credit cards without their knowledge.

In the end, not forgiving them in time. Not only did we break each other's hearts, we broke each other's will…will to care, will to look forward and not back. Ok. Actually, my will.

Eventually I'd leave Long Island, to my parents and worried friends' relief, for Florida.

Fred remarked a few years later: "The best thing for our marriage was you leaving."

Glad I could help. I did exact my revenge. But there was more to come. They had no idea how bad it would eventually get, their public exposure and humiliation. Yes I would get full and irrevocable retribution.

CAPABLE OF BETRAYAL

Chapter 15
Dallas 1989

In one of the shipments was a tape with the title QTS. I put it in the player and saw a young man masturbating. His face was blocked. At the start of the video, no one was there and then the boy entered the shot after apparently turning on the camera. This was a self-made video by one of my teacher's Phillips Exeter Academy students. During a follow-up phone call, I asked Bateman about the whole thing. "I give students video cameras and encourage them to 'let their hair down.'" This is one example of what came back." "I covered his face," my teacher said, "because he [the student] likes to kid me and say: 'You'll go to jail one day!'"

The following week Bateman sent the unedited version of the tape with the boy's face fully revealed. The student looked 14 or 15 years old. He was smiling. He seemed determined to please his teacher.

A few weeks later another tape arrives. Unlike the first tape of the student, this one is not self-made but in fact it is my former teacher who is behind the camera. The Phillips Exeter student looks a bit older, maybe 6-9 months older. He smiles for the camera and obligingly follows Bateman's direction: "Play with yourself. Give us some assplay. Make love to the camera." The student seems to be enjoying himself. But of course, he is. I did too ten years earlier, didn't I? I wondered: Is the student high on weed? Poppers? Wine? He seems relaxed and happy and enjoying himself. It is a highly provocative video. Of course I can't keep my dick my pants. As we both come, I don't know what to think about this. I'm coming here; he's coming there; same teacher directing both of us. Something is wrong, something is off, but I'm still a few years away from seeing the truth. I fervently want to please my teacher. He'd sent me an old video camera with Phillips Exeter Academy inscribed on the side. "Show your partners the camera," Bateman wrote. "All boys want to show off if given the opportunity." Some of my partners agreed and I sent the tapes to Bateman.

Future tapes include filming of Phillips Exeter students in bathrooms and dorm rooms, unbeknownst to them. I really didn't know what to think, other than it was more alarming than titillating. I remembered what Bateman said his 15-year-old Exeter would say:

"You'll go to jail one day!" Still, I fervently wanted to please my teacher and use the Exeter video camera he sent me. In addition to sex with Dallas partners, I'd also send tapes of myself masturbating. Wanting desperately to make my teacher happy and proud of me.

Chapter 16
Dallas-Exeter 1989

I begin dating an older wealthier man in Boston. He flies me from Dallas for a weekend away. I tell him I have a former high school teacher who is head of Drama at Phillips Exeter Academy. Bateman learns of our visit and invites us to Exeter for dinner. At his on-campus residence, I notice at least four large television monitors in his living room and all manner of audio-visual equipment, including multiple computers. Before leaving for dinner, Bateman's student from the video stops by to say hello. He's older than in the videos Bateman sent me, perhaps 18-years-old by now. We chat for a while, but really we're checking each other out. "I wanted to see if you both have chemistry, if you'd like to make a video together." But I didn't get a sense from the student that he was attracted to me. I was around eight years older anyway, more weathered by life. Later at dinner, Bateman was his usual gregarious and funny self, making us all laugh at his mostly sexualized humor.

For myself, this older gentleman from Boston, it would be my final experience in that domain: I had grown tired and weary of this dance, I no longer cared to be adored and deep down only wanted level-playing-field relationships. Frank was now gone. I was no longer the looker I was back in the day. I was ready to hang up my hustler hat.

I eventually realize that my life has been twisted and begin writing about it. I draft a play: "Weaving In & Out" which focuses mostly on the tortured relationship with my mother and her mother. It's quite histrionic but a start at trying to make sense of what's happened in my life. I send it to Bateman. His critique is blunt: not enough structure, not enough drama, "reminds me a bit of 'Glass Menagerie.'" Mostly though his message was: Keep your day job, this is not your gift." Of course I was hurt by the critique, but he was my teacher and a drama god so he must know what he is talking about. I put the play in a drawer but I don't forget about it. As it stews in its hiding place, more aspects of my life stew in my consciousness. What is my psyche trying to tell me? Can I ever put this all together?

CAPABLE OF BETRAYAL

Chapter 17
Dallas 1990

I unexpectantly receive a video cassette and set of Polaroids in the mail from the predator teacher.

Larry Lane Bateman and I had kept contact over the years. Postcards and the occasional phone call. I thought he was my friend. He was vested in me thinking that—and not thinking much more.

The content of the video was quite intense—a mix of adult, teen and kids; I had mixed feelings viewing the tape. I felt queasy seeing the kids and those scenes did not sit well with me.

But I got to wanking right off.

Because that's what you do with such stimulating and provocative material, right?

Furiously masturbate.

Even to the sexually explicit Polaroids of me as a 16-year-old, posing for my teacher, wanting to please him, pleasing him, but the look in my eyes belied a completely different story: vacant, lost, soul-less.

Jerking off!

Morning before work.

After arriving home from the office.

Before bed.

3am as well.

It was never ending, even the chafing and sores on my penis. And I would soon have a lifetime's worth porn.

A week later, I began receiving large packages, each with numerous VHS tapes and picture books. On one hand I found them stimulating; on the other hand, I found some of the material unsettling. I didn't care for prepubescent youth and the images were depressing. But I did like some of the other stuff.

Just like ten years earlier as his student. Some of the experiences I enjoyed, some of it was stimulating, some of it I wanted more of.

I asked him not to send me kids' content. And for a while the arriving boxes just had adult and young adult content. Then I'd find he included kid content in future deliveries, and I'd shake my head and say to myself: "I asked him not to send that stuff."

CAPABLE OF BETRAYAL

After episodes of wanking, I felt an emptiness inside. A hatred of who I was and what I was doing and how I was living my life.

The Gun appeared regularly alongside my right temple.

Every day.

Things at work were becoming untenable for me and them. I was running out of excuses and they were losing patience.

"At what point are you going to stop working the system, Michael?" my boss said. "Patience is running out, mine included."

One day a retail headhunter called my office. My ears perked up. We chatted and after numerous interviews I was hired to join The Limited in Columbus Ohio.

The director of our retail division was beside himself.

"We've made so much progress. You've made progress," he said.

"My time here is over, boss."

My direct supervisor Ted told me he understood why I'd want to leave Dallas. My life had been quite scandalous, not detailed in these pages but can be found in SPILLING THE TEA – *Adventures in a Texas Gay Bar Empire.*

En route to the Midwest and the then cow-town known as Columbus.

I didn't know it at the time but fate did have a few more cards to deal.

Chapter 18
Columbus 1990

Arriving in Columbus, with so much history from Dallas as Frank Caven, gay bar mogul's son and retail career at Neiman Marcus (see SPILLING THE TEA – Book 2 in my memoir anthology, fall 2026), and the real and perceived whispers behind my back, instability run amok, it was a relief to start anew in a new city.

Hello Columbus!

My AA pals would call this a "geographic cure."

And they were right.

A Neiman's office mate confided in me that the consensus was: we can only imagine what chaos he'll bring to The Limited in Ohio.

I learned early on in Columbus, say "Go Bucks" and you have immediate friends. And of course, the urban legend of Ohio's first billionaire The Limited founder Les Wexner.

By now I had developed some skills with numbers and analysis. The Limited's reputation of *working everyone to death* was not unfounded. The merchandising offices were warehouses of burn-out and unhappiness, cubicles of enduring sadness and despair.

But we had a job to do: sell cheap knock-off fashion.

(The Limited's founder Les Wexner was the big boss but really had no idea what we merchandise managers did. I'd hear the name Jeffrey Epstein--who years later would supposedly commit suicide in jail awaiting trial for teen sexual abuse and human trafficking with some very big clients whose secrets he leveraged—bandied about but we had no idea the role Les played in creating that monster, and we all wonder to this day the dirt that Epstein must have on Les for Les to have given him so much money. It's a permanent stain on Les's legacy and all of his charitable and humanitarian work. His wife Abigail is quite detested by most people as she doesn't look people in the eye, as though she's too good or precious to include us mortals in her eyesight. For a while, Mrs. Wexner and I shared the same manicurist and we'd pass by each other between appointments. Honestly I'd never seen a diamond so large in person as the one on Abigal's wedding finger, other than seeing Elizabeth Taylor's fat diamond years earlier at a fundraiser in Washington, DC.)

CAPABLE OF BETRAYAL

The Limited paid well and no one knew my history. *Imposter-chameleon* time again!

After a few weeks in Columbus, settling into the corporate owned apartment and eventually landing a lease on a cute carriage house on Neil Avenue (my Landlord was also my family physician), I made the choice to learn about the Columbus gay bars, especially the Eagle.

What could possibly go wrong?

Drinking, drugging and while passed out…a one-night-stand stole some of my checks from my apartment and forged a few before the bank closed my account.

Word of my unplanned emergency leave of absence from The Limited got back to Derrill.

"Oh I knew—we all knew this would happen," he drawled into my answering machine.

"Godspeed, dear."

Click.

The Limited HR manager offered me time off to do out-patient treatment. My family doctor referred me to a local gay psychologist (there were two to choose from at the time) and I was finally in a financial position to be able to afford the co-pay for therapy.

Not sure how Doc intuited that the psychologist Dr Howard Fradkin would be the best match for me, but he did.

The first few sessions with Howard were to stabilize and review family history. It was gut wrenching as it was the first time I was able share my life in a non-shaming and non-judgmental environment with a gay man in a position of authority who was not trying to make the moves on me.

Years earlier during a psych evaluation at a hospital, the psychiatrist, after hearing my background said, "You're going to have to start over. Be re-parented. It's not easy but much needs to be hollowed out."

Certainly Howard was well positioned to re-parent and as we know I desperately needed it.

In our third session, without any prompting from Howard, I took a deep breath as the realization came crashing down on me.

"Oh my God. He took advantage of me. He's not my friend. Never was."

It was as though the ceiling of his office flew off and I was staring into a bright white light above. I'm shaking and feel I'm losing my breath. The tears flowed then and in subsequent sessions.

"Keep breathing," Howard would say. "This is a safe space." And for the first time, I didn't feel like *an imposter-chameleon*. I can find and be who I really am.

Howard had a long history working with male survivors of sexual abuse and I was in good hands.

We began the hard work of recovery. I returned to the office at The Limited. Lots of whispers and how are you and glad you're back. Soon old news.

Howard recommended male survivor literature and I learned what the word *empowerment* means—and began to see that one day I may be empowered too. But in a meaningful way, not with fucking, objectifying myself or being objectified.

There is a 12-step program for most issues out there. And I found a group at Neil and King Avenues in Columbus called Triple Winners—that combined alcohol, incest and food recovery. The group became a bedrock of my early recovery.

After a draining week at The Limited, each Friday late afternoon I'd make the long walk down Neil Avenue to the Holy Trinity Community Church listening to REM's "Happy, Shiny People" on my Walkman.

One evening a fellow group member Lisa brought the guy she was dating—tall, blonde and a majestic nose fit for a king! We locked eyes – his eyes intense grey -- and I immediately wondered if she knew her guy was bisexual?!

The following week I went to a different meeting—AA only—and there he was again *sans* Lisa. We made potent eye contact and I hustled over to introduce myself and exchange numbers. Tom was surprised at my forwardness and smiled slightly.

"Yeah, let's go for coffee sometime."

So would begin our journey.

When we met again, Tom disrobed and I nearly fainted. It's not that I haven't seen large members in the past, and in fact Texas is full of little guys at 5' 6" with dicks swinging down to their knees.

But to take in this 6'5" blond adonis with his extremely large penis took my breath away!

CAPABLE OF BETRAYAL

What they say about big feet and big hands is true!

It should be designated a national monument.

(I gave Tom an advance copy of this memoir to read and tell me anything he'd wanted taken out. He was fine with everything, including the big hands and feet bit. I always knew Tom was secretly proud of his big German American cock! Thankfully Tom was not discovered by the gay porn industry. He certainly would have been a living legend.)

Although Tom had had scattered same-sex experiences in earlier years, he neither looked or dressed gay, did not identify as gay and after our energetic post-coffee romp in the sack, Tom put on his clothes and looked down in shame.

"I do not want this. I am not this."

He quickly left, and I was convinced that we would never see each other again.

Thankfully I was wrong.

Tom and I shared immaculate joy in the early days of our relationship.

I'd always separated emotions from sexual intimacy; with Tom, I let go and kissing, hugging and holding took on a world of their own, a universe of foreverness.

He was the first man I could ever imagine growing old with. Looking into his eyes of discovery at his awakened life felt like a privilege. And it was.

Tom was very brave. His family had no idea, friends had no idea and Tom was unsure but open-minded. Tom has this thing called *integrity* — and even back then as his being transformed, Tom was committed to living a life based on truth of self.

But it would not be easy.

We became inseparable other than our respective work lives, moving in together and setting up house. It was wondrous to be in a same-age relationship and on a level playing field with such a gorgeous hunk-a hunk of burning love.

Our love and passion burned brightly, baby.

On Valentine's Day Tom was waiting for me after work…on the bed in my small carriage house.

When I walked up the spiral stairway to our loft bedroom, there he was butt naked and somehow had been able to put whip cream in the shape of a valentine on his back.

I licked ravenously.

It's good that the carriage house was not connected to any other building. Else the shaking, pounding and hollering would be a nuisance.

Soon thereafter we were tested for HIV. With negative statuses we were able to enjoy condom-free lovemaking. It was joyous.

And our helpful general practitioner prescribed a special ointment that numbed me so on the rare occasions Tom wanted to top, I didn't have to worry about being destroyed and never walking again! Thank you, Dr Feelgood!

Part of Tom's gay 101 also meant an introduction to Broadway show-tunes. I mean, Hello!

On Saturday mornings we'd blast "I Am What I Am!" and join in at the top of our lungs. Our neighbors did hear all that and commented in passing, "How sweet!"

Tom began coming out to family members. With a Catholic background I expected resistance from his family—but they were accepting and open. Of course, Tom's mother suspected (as many mothers do) but the rest of his family was floored.

This was the family I had dreamed of—parents who were able to look at their respective pasts and ways they were there for their kids—and ways they let them down. Everyone was focused on self-discovery and growth. What a dream! And I was welcomed with open arms and felt at home, *imposter-chameleon* be damned. It was so different from any family situation I'd ever seen or experienced, other than Maribeth's surrogate family in Great Neck when I was a kid.

"Is there something you wanna tell me?" asked Tom's longtime friend and college roommate.

Tom and I had returned from the 1992 LGBT March on Washington, his face was half red from being outside (we were honored to march alongside civil rights icon Jessie Jackson and gay rights icon David Mixner).

"You were in Washington DC last weekend, right?"

CAPABLE OF BETRAYAL

And so, Tom took the big step and came out to his suspecting BFF Kevin.

Tom came out to ALL his colleagues at the family business. They too were floored. At the annual awards banquet, all eyes were on me and Tom sitting side-by-side. I suppose it helped that the banquet serving line wound around our table. We just kept chatting comfortably. The following year's award banquet…we were *old news.*

A pal from Atlanta told me: "Michael, you sure are marrying well." That was true at all levels.

In therapy I was making progress. The anger that I had pressed downward for so long was coming up—in healthy and safe ways. The heaviness in my chest, the overall depression—was naturally lifting.

I came to see how the teacher had used, abused and manipulated me.

I had wanted to please him so much—at 16 as well as an adult.

There was so much to unpack in therapy. In the early months I went 3 times a week, thankful for the insurance and my new financial ability to meet co-pays.

I kept journaling and writing and eventually revealed my whole story to Tom.

Of course Tom had never heard anything like it and was fascinated and repulsed by the awful parts of my story. But I told him everything and my deep fear that he'd break it off didn't happen. In fact, Tom embraced me, baggage and all. Again, *imposter-chameleon* be damned.

One concern in therapy: what to do about Maribeth and Fred? During visits with them I found myself very depressed afterward. With the realizations in therapy, the entire relationship felt untenable. In fact, I sent them a letter for the ages. It was scathing and eliminated any possibility of a reunion. The letter I sent them was a true weapon of destruction.

Maribeth, Fred and I were broken beyond measure.

Another ongoing issue in therapy was Bateman's porn collection that was still in my hands.

What would I do?

Go to the dumpster and be rid of it all and the teacher?

(There were two gay psychologists in Columbus at the time. Knowing the other one, I am sure he would have counseled for the dumpster. Howard didn't counsel either way).

Contact the police?

And what about the teacher Larry Lane Bateman and the people in his life, especially his partner Hal Lynch who worked at Phillips Exeter Academy as well?

Howard suggested I seek counsel from a local family attorney, and I did.

After I told the attorney everything, she asked, "What do you want?"

"I want him removed from the education system," I said. "I don't want him to do to more boys what he did to me."

"Okay," the attorney replied, "Here's how."

The plan was a lot to take in. Because it would mean 100% public exposure. The teacher would have the right to face his accuser in court and for me to be questioned by his defense attorney. We all know that many victims of sexual abuse avoid the courts for that simple reason—being re-traumatized, being exposed, losing standing in the community and with their families.

It was a lot to ruminate on and I didn't take it lightly. Many sessions with Howard, many chats with Tom. Both Tom and Howard were clear: it's your decision, follow your heart, there is no right or wrong and we will support you and believe in you—no matter what.

Finally I made the decision—to do *the right thing*, consequences and exposure be damned. I'm gonna take my power back from that person who took advantage of me so badly when I was 16.

My Columbus family attorney got everything in motion. I'd be turning in all the materials to the New Hampshire authorities and testifying that the teacher shipped them to me via the postal service. These are state (and perhaps federal) crimes. The key to the approach was securing an immunity from prosecution in New Hampshire, which the attorney did.

After numerous conversations between the district attorney and my family attorney, the immunity was obtained and I flew to New Hampshire to be interviewed by the police.

I met with the District Attorney at the time Carleton Eldridge and an Exeter Police detective.

CAPABLE OF BETRAYAL

I gave multiple statements. One of the issues at hand concerned a videotape Bateman had sent me of a 15-year-old Phillips Exeter student.

[The former student has gone to extensive lengths throughout this drama to shield his identity from public view. In these pages I will respect his wish to be anonymous and refer to him only as A. A is not his first, middle or last initial.]

The detective collected Phillips Exeter Academy yearbooks and soon enough we identified **A**.

(Years later **A** and Bateman's partner Hal Lynch, who amazingly kept his job at Exeter, would collide in a rather public way. More later.)

On a subsequent trip to New Hampshire, I testified before the grand jury (the case had been moved to the federal level).

Police launched search warrants on the teacher's campus apartment. What they found was no surprise but rocked the Phillips Exeter Academy and led to national media coverage. With so many current and former students coming from famous families, the scuttlebutt was: who's in the videos?

Eventually my identity would be revealed and my name would go on the record.

There was no turning back.

Everything would change—yet again.

Chapter 19
New Hampshire 1991-92

Tom and I were in New York for a short summer holiday and weekend with friends Phillip and Daniel at their place in the Hamptons.

En route back to NYC we drove past my old house on Long Island.

Tom couldn't get his arms around the fact that we wouldn't be stopping by to say hello to Maribeth and Fred.

Back in NYC, we picked up the Sunday Times and there was a short article about porn being found at a New Hampshire prep schoolteacher's on-campus apartment.

That was a trickle.

But the spigot was about to overflow in the days and weeks ahead.

The media would soon report the predator teacher Larry Lane Bateman was covertly videotaping male students in the dormitory bathrooms.

During my interviews with the police, district attorney and eventually US Assistant Attorney I was totally upfront about my past.

I was committed to avoiding any surprises about me, the main witness. I disclosed all elements of my past that any defense attorney would try to capitalize on.

Except...the teacher's defense attorney, who took out an ad in the Texas gay press for anyone to respond with info on me. They had to have been sorely disappointed when their inquiries led to nothing new. No smoking gun. Whatever they found out I'd already disclosed in police interviews and grand jury testimony.

A legal defense fund was started for the teacher. Being extremely popular, numerous past and current students' families contributed. "People, I'm innocent! I need your help," he'd write in an appeal letter.

Around the same time, Tom and I decided that I would return to school and work towards a master's in psychology and social work. Retail was draining me and was not my gift. It was time to move-on.

With some time off before the trial, I was able to mentally prepare for the road ahead. I knew it would be bumpy.

CAPABLE OF BETRAYAL

"It's so messy, Mike-o!" Granchar said about the whole thing. She explained her one niece and two nephews said that a "wonderful teacher lost his career because of you. It's awful!"

"They said that?" I exclaimed. "After what he did to me, him losing his career is more important to them?"

She could hear my face redden over the phone.

After a moment: "Yes I'll eat crow. You're right. Just so hard to take in. Oh Mike-o, yes you're doing the right thing, but so did Jesus and look what they did to him."

I remembered my Granchar's stories of Grandpomp's days as a judge and earlier as a public defender. He hated representing guilty people and getting them off on technicalities. But that was what you did in law—represent people who you don't like or care for because everyone deserves a robust defense.

And I'd read plenty of Perry Mason as a kid (from my late grandfather's collection) and my main take-away: no matter what, keep your cool on the stand.

Even though I have always been pro-prosecution, I was wise enough to know that not all defense attorneys are bad and not all prosecutors are good.

As the teacher's trial approached, I rejected all media requests to avoid distraction and inconsistencies in personal comments and upcoming testimony.

I met a few times with a local Columbus spiritualist. She worked with some of Tom's family. Aware of what I was facing, her message was prescient. "Michael, what you're facing will test you at all levels. But unlike most people, you know your shadow self, you know there are multiple dimensions to your character and personality, else you wouldn't be who you are today. You're choosing a road less traveled, for sure. Ever read the book?" I nodded. "Good. Recently I saw an ad for a movie about Malcolm X in a magazine. He was complicated, like you." She pulled out the magazine and turned to the advertisement: "Malcolm X: Scholar, Convict, Leader, Hipster, Father, Hustler, Minister, Black man. Every man." Michael, you are many varied things—embrace them and yourself. Father-mother God blessings for what's ahead."

My family attorney dropped me a card in the mail: "You are one brave guy," she wrote.

A few days before I left Ohio for New Hampshire we received a list of witnesses for the defense, which included a who's who of people from my Dallas days, including Denis, my longtime nemesis I'd hoped to have left behind.

He must have been very excited.

I quietly arrived at Concorde New Hampshire and was housed at a hotel outside of town to avoid media and anyone else.

Although the judge was also housed at the same hotel (brought in from Puerto Rico given the high profile of the case), I knew better than to speak with him. I'd see him having breakfast with his female clerks. I had a sense that something wasn't right with that guy. But I couldn't put my finger on it.

In the stuffy federal courtroom that first morning the place was packed and I was beyond nervous. Every public viewing row full. Lots of press. All eyes on me.

I felt prepared. I knew my former teacher's defense attorney would try to rattle me.

And he did try.

Waving around sexually explicit polaroids of 16-year-old me that my teacher had taken years earlier on Long Island at a special "away-from-school" video project at his house.

I refused to be provoked, although it certainly was a disgusting display. This type of courtroom conduct is something all victims come to expect when dealing with defense attorneys who represent accused sexual criminals.

I told myself to keep breathing. Over and over in my head, I affirmed: *Just do this. You'll get through it. You'll get to the other side.*

When I took the stand on the first day, I was visibly shaking. The judge proffered a glass of water from a nearby table, which I took. Again, hand shaking.

I'd never been so scared in my life.

I was required to identify the teacher, which I did. "That's him." I raised my arm and pointed to Larry Lane Bateman. I suppose he'd been practicing his angry face for a while. And indeed, he looked scary and angry.

I took it in and moved on. It was difficult but made sure that I was ok looking at him and not allowing his mind-games to get to me.

Goodness knows his mind-games were quite effective when I was his teenage high school student on Long Island.

Remember the sex predator mantra: "You're crazy. You're lying. It never happened."

That's what he tried to convey with his raging glare.

And the jury was confronted with two possibilities: either I was a victim of this teacher or I had victimized the teacher as a dastardly hustler. Which would they choose? Would they believe me or him? Would they take any opportunity to question my credibility and acquit the teacher of at least one count, as his attorney begged them to?

"I'm not completely stupid," the teacher said during testimony. "I gave Michael the porn, I didn't ship it to him."

I was allowed to sit in on closing arguments a few days later.

Behind me sat one of my teacher's most vocal advocates, a former high school classmate. She kept whispering, "No, no, no" during the prosecution's summation and "yes, yes, yes" during the defense summation. At the conclusion of closing arguments, she whispered in my ear, "You're a liar. We all know it. You know it." And she stood up and made a hasty exit.

I returned to the prosecutor's office awaiting the verdict, closed the door to an inner conference room, sat down and wept. Guttural sobs. If I could puke up my guts I would. Because they ached. I felt naked, exposed, even permanently compromised. I could no longer be the *imposter-chameleon.* The enormity of public exposure hit me, people knowing stuff about me I'd long wished would be able to stay in the dustbin of my chaotic younger adult years—but had to come out if this man was to be permanently removed from the education system.

Would the jury believe me? Would the jury throw Bateman a bone? How would I ever be able to go on with a normal life, no matter what the outcome?

The tears that ran down my face burned with the realization that nothing would be the same again.

Michael Caven

Chapter 20
Columbus-New Hampshire 1992

After the government concluded its case, it was the defense's turn and time to see what, if any defense can be mounted against all the damning physical evidence, including the actual boxes that Bateman sent me the materials in. Including the polaroids he'd taken when I was his 16-year-old student.

From his arrest to the courtroom, Team Bateman consistently chattered on about homophobia and discrimination by the authorities. Yet in all my interactions with the police, district attorney, federal prosecutors, I never saw or experienced any homophobia or anti-gay bias. I was treated only with respect and compassion.

There was much chatter among the government attorneys about Bateman's defense strategy. The prosecutors looked at the teacher's attorney as a Jack Kevorkian figure—leading the path to the teacher's demise.

The only reason Bateman didn't plea out was to see what would happen with me at the trial—would I show up? Would I be a reliable witness or bonkers? The teacher, his allies and attorney were hoping for the worst.

I let them down.

The point was not only to get him off but to punish me. Expose me. Make me sorry for turning in my teacher, for revealing the abuse, for not staying loyal to my perpetrator.

By staying focused and keeping my eye on the prize—Bateman's permanent removal from the education system—I certainly let them down and didn't give Bateman and his allies what they hoped for.

My testimony from the grand jury to the trial held up and stayed consistent. Seeing Denis and his cohorts plus some old high school classmates ready to undermine my testimony—nothing got under my skin and in fact their presence made me more determined.

Their strategy did not pay off, including bringing in my longtime nemesis Denis Weir.

Another glorious day for Denis.

Or what is?

Although I sat through final arguments, I was unable to view the balance of the trial, other than my own participation.

Court onlookers would tell me later than Denis showed up in an expensive bespoke suit with plenty of bling, and of course his garish gold rimmed eyeglasses.

The prosecutor listened as Denis testified under questioning from the teacher's attorney. Michael this, Michael that. A bad guy who tried to get people to stop drinking. Didn't do much in Washington DC while at JR's. Denis even accused me of being a sex offender.

Under cross by the government, Denis acknowledged that I really wasn't a bad guy after all. He acknowledged how he benefitted financially from Frank's estate.

I'm told jurors just rolled their eyes.

Other former students testified, including **A**, the former student who was 15 or 16 when Bateman videotaped him masturbating and Bateman performing oral sex and anilingus on him.

A and I crossed paths in one of the court hallways. I said hello and he just looked at me with a sense of befuddlement mixed with sadness. My understanding was he did not want to testify, his family hired a very expensive attorney; still he was on the hook to testify that the predator teacher filmed him and sexually abused him when he was a teenager.

Another high school classmate of mine, Beth, testified that I had told her back in 1980 what had happened at the teacher's Long Island home.

On the defense side, a few former students testified on Bateman's behalf. One, Hal Lynch, testified that it was he, not Bateman, who led the seduction when they were teacher-student at Interlochen Center for the Arts.

You can make of that what you will.

There were 4 indictments for the teacher. The defense hammered one of them, one that totally depended on my testimony. If the jury would just find him not guilty of that one, it would convey that they didn't totally believe me. The defense practically begged the jury to throw him a bone. If the jury didn't find me totally credible, it was their opportunity to collectively say so.

CAPABLE OF BETRAYAL

The jury did not bite and found the teacher guilty of all charges. The jury believed me. The teacher and his allies—their plan did not work.

After the 1-week trial and a Friday afternoon verdict, jurors chatted with me and wished me the best, some offering hugs. Bateman was released on his current bond. I returned to Ohio vindicated but the story wasn't yet over.

On my way back to Ohio after the trial, I laid over in NYC and met with Jesse Kornbluth, a writer for Tina Brown's Vanity Fair.

I was optimistic as previous Vanity Fair stories about teacher-student sexual abuse had been covered fairly and were actually somewhat enlightened.

But not in this case.

I know, it did not help that my background was so salacious.

Unbeknownst to me, their angle would be that somehow the poor pedophile predator teacher had been victimized by former student turned dastardly hustler. And the magazine made a deal to get the teacher's early cooperation: leave out accounts of his victimizing other teenage boys, including his surreptitious videotaping of Exeter boys while showering and changing in the dormitory bathrooms.

And create a mystery. *A mystery that did not exist.* The article purposefully and erroneously inferred that Bateman did not own a video camera in 1979. Of course he did.

It was pretty crafty.

So, I got interviewed by this guy not knowing that the article would be a sympathetic portrait of a pedophile molester.

But there were red flags.

"I've fucked a lot of people," Jessie Kornbluth opened the interview while we had lunch at iconic Café Un Deux Trois on 44th Street. He should have added: *And I'm about to fuck you.* And really, the comment, if it was an attempt to bond with me, was silly. Everybody in New York City fucks a lot, I mean hello.

Kornbluth went on to mansplain his definition of victimization and proceeded to share a sad story about an African American women being robbed and beat up. "That's a victim," he said.

Uh-oh, I'm thinking, this guy is fully on Team Bateman, I don't stand a chance. I considered ending the interview but was too far in, and still hopeful that I could educate this man (I did send him some literature on male sexual abuse survivorship.)

Kornbluth also disclosed that he was storing a pornography collection for a friend from Fire Island in his Manhattan apartment closet. Was he baiting me to turn him in to the authorities? Really, what was wrong with this guy?

On the lighter side, during that stopover in New York, I came upon a gift shop with a card section. "Happy Father's Day," read one card. The inside description: *I love father's so much, I decided to have several.* A welcome laugh to an otherwise stressful situation.

A few months later I returned to New Hampshire for the teacher's sentencing hearing. Different than the trial, the court heard from experts in pedophilia and child abuse. I testified about my family life and more details relating to the teacher's abuse.

In fact, Bateman's sentencing hearing became an indictment of my relationship with my mother.

My testimony did not sit well with the judge, Jose Fuste, who despite my initial misgivings had run what appeared to be a good trial a few months earlier.

Perhaps he saw me as disloyal to my parents. I don't know. But he laid into me in his comments—stating he didn't believe everything I said, questioned my motives for coming forward and that the teacher and I were *two peas in a pod.*

Yikes.

Fuste was offended. He asked questions. He wanted more. Did she [Maribeth] perform oral sex on you? I don't know. I don't remember. Note I did not say yes because I honestly don't remember.

But apparently you believed me enough to convict, right Judge?

Took me a while to unpack that and his ignorant comments.

Afterward, I wrote him a letter and asked if he preferred I stayed silent? I reminded him that when I was 16 and the teacher was in a position of trust and betrayed it.

He did not respond but it was entered into the court record.

Years later the judge would leave the bench under a dark cloud of sexual harassment claims by his female clerks.

Due to the elite status of Phillips Exeter academy, there was a lot of national media coverage. Most of it was spot-on and accurate.

CAPABLE OF BETRAYAL

Except of course for Tina Brown's treatment and the attempt to clumsily tie together homosexuality and pedophilia, a sad old trope.

Eventually bloggers would take the approach apart, one calling it a "whitewashing" of Bateman, the other "pedophilia chic." Another story, in the Washington Examiner, states that the Vanity Fair article's chief victim was Larry Lane Bateman, and that Kornbluth wrote, "probably the most heartfelt and sympathetic portrayal of a convicted child pornography trafficker yet to appear in print." Further, "not a kind or empathetic word for the man who claimed to have been abused by Bateman as a teenager…if Bateman's cache of pornography featured little girls, rather than little boys, it is unthinkable that he would have become the object of a sympathetic profile in the likes of Vanity Fair."

In fact, the writer seethed with fury and if honest would have said, "How dare you take down such a fine academic?" In the spirit of sex predators, he accommodated—take down the accuser. I strongly believe that in Kornbluth's perverted view of things, he considered Bateman and I consenting adults when I was 16.

A sloppy piece that attempted to create a mystery that didn't exist while misrepresenting one source as two different people.

Jesse Kornbluth even asked me if I had AIDS/HIV. Perhaps he wanted to add "Death Wish" to his "Dastardly Hustler" POV. No, I don't have HIV/AIDS. *And fuck you cunt for even asking.*

Perhaps the folks at Vanity Fair saw Bateman's 1980 out-of-school vile sexually explicit video project with me as *avant garde?*

My silence would be a complicity with Bateman and my parents. Silence would certainly mean no haters and privacy maintained. So why? Because as AIDS activists would say: silence equals death. And in my case (and the case of any sex abuse victim), silence definitely means shame and possibly death, if not an actual death, a living death.

In this case, Vanity Fair was on the wrong side of history.

After its publication, Kornbluth told me: "It could have been a lot worse."

"For you or for me?" would be my response today.

A friend who read the VF article recently, responded: "That never would have made it to print in 2025."

Whether media coverage or an ignorant judge, a few angry classmates who would defend the teacher no matter what—none of it changed the reality of the outcome—a sex predator teacher was permanently removed from the education system.

Male victim-survivors scored a victory.

They won.

I won.

A predator teacher was held to account and nothing anyone could say or do would change that fact.

This was the most *important* thing I would ever accomplish in my life.

The day after the dressing down by the judge, I returned to Ohio and began a Psychology-Social Work Master of Science program and the rest of my life.

Bruised but victorious.

Still the Vanity Fair article rankled me. I felt it set back the progress of the LGBT movement and damaged it by connecting pedophilia and homosexuality. I hoped one day to be able to bring a better story to the LGBT cultural landscape.

It took months to come to terms with the trial, the sentencing and the aftermath of emotions.

On one hand, it was fantastic—a victory for me and male survivors.

On the other hand, I felt raw and exposed. I deeply regretted attending the sentencing hearing (other than seeing Bateman being led away in handcuffs, which the prosecutors and I watched intently and with satisfaction) and participating in some of the media—Vanity Fair specifically.

Larry Lane Bateman was going to jail, in my mind and heart, for what he did to me when I was 16. Yes child porn is bad and victims are permanently enshrined in their respective traumas by pictures that never age and forever show evidence of the perpetration, including the underage Polaroids my teacher took of me...languishing in FBI files in Quantico and god know who's buried collection somewhere, the irony not lost on anyone that one of the counts against him—that he was found guilty of—was transporting the Polaroids he made of me when I was 16-years-old. Bateman was led away with his liberty and freedom removed *quid pro quo* for his selfish actions at the away-from-school video at his Long Island home. The pornography was a vehicle toward accountability and punishment. I regret not one bit of it.

(Now let me take the opportunity to speak directly to Hal Lynch, A and anyone else in Larry Lane Bateman's orbit: your pal Bateman was in numerous chat rooms—which started in 1989—before his arrest. The rooms for pedophiles were also populated by FBI agents. It was a matter of time before Bateman was ensnared, and you can be sure that anyone that Bateman had regular contact with would be vulnerable to search & seizure; the FBI wouldn't care if you were a former student and victim, partner or collaborator. So guys, it could and probably would have been worse for all of us had I not turned in Bateman the way I did. Let that soak in for a while.)

Let's tie up some loose ends:

Mother Maribeth passed away, in Fred's arms according to the obituary. I read about it on the internet. I didn't feel a thing and still don't. I had come to terms that I'd never see Maribeth or Fred again. A few years earlier Fred had sent a letter and pictures before my final confrontation letter. He wrote: "You'll always have a family." Was he tone deaf? **Fred for being totally in denial about what a family *is* and the limits of my loyalty. Or me, being callous and cruel—I tore up his pictures and that of his family. As the ink paper ripped, it was the death nell. There would never be a reconciliation now; with some wisdom and maturity…I wish I could have delivered some back then. But wishful thinking never accomplished a fucking thing.** Fred retired and passed away in a care facility surrounded by big bushes, to keep onlookers and outsiders away.

I'm hoping that Maribeth is riding on her girlfriend Ree's motorbike throughout heaven, most importantly being who she is without apology or rationalizations.

onto Phillips Exeter Academy.

The story did not end with the predator-teacher's conviction and incarceration in 1993.

After the trial I obtained all the court transcripts as material for my then planned memoir. Interesting reading. I wasn't capable of telling and showing the story as I've been able to do here. It was 30 years ago and that version of me simply didn't have the ability. Hopefully that's different now.

I was flabbergasted when reading the testimony of Bateman's defense witnesses. One, a comedian named Jim David was a triple threat—not funny, not helpful and not bright. Another of the witnesses, Hal Lynch, a former Interlochen Arts student and current at-the-time domestic partner (who also taught at Exeter) testified that it was he, not Bateman, who was the seducer in their relationship: when he was his student, he says he threw himself at Bateman for sex, according to his testimony.

I assumed that Phillips Exeter Academy had reps at the trial and heard this and other testimony. I imagined that perhaps they'd take some action after hearing what the teacher and his allies testified about.

But nothing.

Every few years I'd google and see that the teacher's partner Hal continued to teach and advance at Exeter. I found this surprising. Unless of course Exeter didn't witness the trial. Or perhaps just didn't care.

Years later, the trustees of Phillips Exeter Academy launched an independent investigation of all known instances of teacher/staff-student sexual abuse and inappropriate relationships. The independent third party did an exhaustive investigation and of course my teacher's case was included.

During their investigation, they read Hal's testimony as well as his role (as an alleged bystander) in the Bateman's sexual abuse of a 15-year-old Phillips Exeter Academy student.

The student, identified in these pages as **A** to preserve his anonymity, had also been interviewed by the investigators.

At the conclusion of the investigation and with recommendations in hand for each case (around 10 in total over the last 50 years…that are known about) Phillips Exeter Academy fired Bateman's partner Hal Lynch, saying that he should have intervened and stopped the abuse of the teenage Exeter student in the late 1980's.

After 25 years of Exeter employment and advancement, Hal was out. And very unhappy. He launched a wrongful termination lawsuit against Phillips Exeter, contending he was fired because he was gay and because he testified at the predator-teacher's trial. He steadfastly denied knowing of the abuse of the 15-year-old. But **A** would write anonymously to the Exeter community *that he had to know.* Phillips

CAPABLE OF BETRAYAL

Exeter settled **A** with a nice fat check and the 25-year Exeter veteran lost his case. The judge on the civil matter did not believe him.

Larry Lane Bateman died in 2014.

***

After Bateman's trial, I struggled with night terrors and early one morning ran into an open door while half asleep and in terror.

In the upcoming months, when he sensed a night terror episode was coming, Tom would wrap his arms around me to keep me from lunging out of our bed.

I'd see an apparition of my mother at the end of the bed, seemingly as real as the day is long. "Do you see it?" I'd yell to Tom, who of course didn't because nothing was there, except in my terror.

Tom.

How can I not mention my bedrock before, during and after New Hampshire?

Tom was so proud of me and continually praised my courage and fortitude. How lucky I was to have his support and his family's support.

My master's degree coursework involved late afternoon and evening classes. We graduate students were encouraged to work in mental health and I landed a job as a social worker during day-time hours.

Over time the drama of New Hampshire faded from my mind and I moved on. I found psychology to be fascinating and my new social work clients—all severely mentally disabled—kept me on my toes.

One of my practicums took place at the same mental health center where I worked.

Different department though.

Sex offenders. Yikes again.

And I was good at the work although found the clients to be challenging. Most were court mandated, highly narcissistic and varying levels of psychopathy.

In mental health, alcohol and drug counseling tends to be confrontative. Even more so for sex offenders. Breaking down the ego and trying to shine the light of victim empathy—these are important goals in sex offender treatment.

And rarely reached.

I earned my master's within 2 years and a 4.0 overall GPA.

Much different than my roller-coaster grades from SMU.

If ever there was a bipolar undergraduate transcript, it was my SMU transcript.

The sex offender program director liked my clinical skills and offered a position after graduation. I took the job but hated it and the clients. Still, I did my best and tried to break through.

I did around 100 assessments during my tenure.

After a while, with the male pedophile clients, I came to expect the disclosure of a female relative, female babysitter or any female in a position of power having somehow sexually offended the client. I'm not saying that all male pedophiles have been sexually abused by women in power but I found it to be a dominating theme in their histories.

Now you may be thinking: Didn't your babysitter and mom offend you, Michael? Yes they did. Based on my childhood, based on the materials that the predator teacher exposed me to, yes all the math adds up to pedophilia.

But I am not a pedophile. I am not sexually attracted to prepubescent kids. I don't know why. Just like I don't know why I didn't get AIDS or get killed in all the dangerous situations I put myself in.

But I'm not and I'm grateful.

CAPABLE OF BETRAYAL

Chapter 21
Columbus Ohio 1993

Tom and I would bring our life partnership full circle with a Commitment Ceremony in 1994. Back in the early '90's same-sex marriage was not yet illegal. We wanted to make a public statement about our union. The special day included all of Tom's family, my Granchar, who stood up for me and close friends. We catered the event at the Delaware Cultural Arts Center (north of Columbus) with full meal, drag show with local icon Shante Seville (Granchar spent a lot of time in Shante's dressing room, vodka and cigs and many questions for her new friend and appreciation for her make-up and costumes), music and dancing. Attendees had never been to a Commitment Ceremony; yet perhaps they found more common ground than they expected. Two people who love each other and want to spend the rest of their lives together. Simple. Easy to understand. As one of our friends said, "I hope my future spouse looks at me the way you and Tom look at each other—with such radiant love."

We'd honeymoon in the South of France, from one end of Cote de Azur to the other.

CAPABLE OF BETRAYAL

Chapter 22
Columbus & Richmond Hill 1993

My Nana in Queens would eventually pass away.

As we've seen, my Sicilian Nana and I had a complicated and tortured relationship. When I was a kid, she'd say she wanted me to grow up to be a women's hair stylist. Nana felt that was my calling. Perhaps it was my effeminate nature. Although she would deny to her death that I was gay.

We had a falling out a few years earlier. And carried on the family tradition of what is now known as "ghosting".

But we did try for a reconciliation and had a few phone chats. I'd be in New York the following week and yes I'd drop by Richmond Hill, Queens, for a visit.

I sent her a postcard: I'll be arriving this Saturday morning.

That Saturday, I called from a pay phone when I was an hour out. No answer. I tried again a half hour out. No answer. I called cousin Shirley and her son answered.

"Go to Muriel's, Michael. It's bad."

Shaking and crying and trying not to hit any cars, I saw an ambulance pulling away from the curb in front of Nana's brownstone.

"Do you have my Nana?" I screamed.

"Go to the house," the paramedic said with resignation.

Nana was sitting upright in her master bedroom chair. Dead of course. But a view of a picture of her beloved mother, the last thing she saw.

Cousin Shirley was hysterical, screaming and crying. It felt like an Italian opera. I kneeled down and took my Nana's cold hand. My tears dropped on them and I too began to wail.

What was supposed to be a joyful (ok joyful is pushing it) reunion became a death scene of operatic proportions.

After calling the funeral home (of course Nana had prepaid her coffin, mausoleum space, and funeral service), the mortician took Nana away and the tears followed her all the way down to the hearse.

Why that morning?

CAPABLE OF BETRAYAL

One of Nana's biggest lifelong fears was that she would die and not be discovered in her Queens brownstone. She was terrified at the thought of decaying for weeks on end.

She knew I was coming.

It was the perfect time to die.

Cousin Shirley would manage the estate and her sons benefitted as did I.

We honored the stipulation in her Will that Maribeth not be invited or allowed at her funeral. Nana could not countenance Maribeth looking down at her in the coffin.

I met with the funeral home make-up artist who would create Nana's final face. I wanted her beautiful for eternity. I knew the shade of lipstick Nana preferred—a deep red. The make-up artist allowed me to join her to get Nana's make-up as perfect as possible. Could we make it as glorious as Nancy Reagan's hairdresser Robin Weir did during Nana's make-over a few years earlier in Washington DC? We did our best. And Nana absolutely glowed in her coffin and wrapped in her beloved mink stole.

We insured that Nana's coffin send-off included a bottle of vodka, a case of cigarettes, photo of the both of us, her hair-buns, and a ceramic imitation of a Boston Terrier—her cherished dog Willie. We sprayed her favorite Chanel perfume in her final resting boudoir just as it was being closed forever.

Years earlier we'd go visit her pre-paid Queens mausoleum space and sit on the bench and stair up at it. (The spaces higher up were not as expensive. Nana was frugal with everything except vodka and cigs…and she loved how her passive income from annuities paid for all of it.) Later we'd head to Woodlawn Cemetery and visit her mom.

She'd bring white paint and make sure her mom's name and dates were sparkly white. Also, a picnic basket. We'd have lunch and she'd chat with her dead mother. Always the conversation ended with Nana saying, "I'm sorry. Forgive me, Mama."

Much regret.

I regretted sending Nana a confrontation letter years earlier where I took her apart piece by piece.

I regretted judging her. Condemning her for being a high price call girl, for aborting my Aunts and Uncles, for refusing to get help for her drinking, for the rage that she and Mom shared. I regretted it all.

And it was too late to change it, take it back or at least make amends. She could have cut me out of her Will. I expected it.

But deep down she loved her little Flip.

No matter what.

When was I going to learn to stop sending angry letters?

Write them.

But don't fucking mail them.

Eventually I would learn.

Tom and I would be in a different financial position due to Nana's generous inheritance.

We'd always wanted to do a business together. Perhaps now we could make that dream come true.

Chapter 23
Columbus, Ohio 1995

"I wonder what would happen if famous gays and lesbians from different historical time periods met, what would they say to each other?"

And so begins the Out On Main Restaurant story, the USA's first LGBT themed restaurant celebrating gay culture and history.

Although Tom and I were co-founders, the original idea came from me one afternoon when I asked Tom the question above.

Our fortunes would change at various times during our relationship—this was the first time—with Nana's inheritance.

So we began to dream.

First we considered the LGBT restaurant, bar and nightclub landscape in Columbus, Ohio in 1995.

There was one gay restaurant—the beloved Grapevine, a casual joint that had been around seemingly forever.

And there were the usual assortment of gay bars, lesbian bars and mixed   nightclubs.
But all of them were hidden away. No windows, minimal signage, in the shadows typical of gay businesses in the Midwest at the time.

We wanted to change that.

With our respective backgrounds in food and hospitality, we believed we brought enough to the table to open a restaurant. But we knew that there was a lot we didn't know. So we'd need to bring in talent.

Back to our coterie of historical LGBT's...

Imagining Alexander the Great, Gertrude Stein, Willa Cather, Oscar Wilde, Alberta Hunter, Cole Porter, Tennessee Williams, Eleanor Roosevelt all together at a Round Table on the Main Stage—what stories would they share, where would they agree and disagree?

Of course that's all projection and motivating insofar as giving a examples of empowerment—that LGBT's have had influential places in history from the beginning of time.

In the 1980's and 1990's theme restaurants were very popular in the US and other parts of the world. Hard Rock Cafe, Planet Hollywood—to name the most well-known and popular.

It was 1995. We began to consider a gay version, a gay Planet Hollywood. Aware of the rich yet tortured history of LGBT people, we wanted to create a setting that celebrated our history in culture, entertainment and everyday life.

But an eclectic design does not guarantee great food and service. We had a lot to do.

The location was chosen for us.

Tom's family owned a percentage of a restaurant space in downtown Columbus. The previous occupant made its international reputation by filing a lawsuit against a couple who were no-show's for a New Year's Eve dinner. Made worldwide press for its audacity, especially during a time when there had been a focus amongst restauranteurs to up the game of customer service.

The 100+ year old mixed use building was at 122 E Main Street—restaurant on ground floor; separate business and bar in the basement; offices on the upper floors; exposed brick and high ceilings throughout.

We bought out Tom's parents' interest.

Although the location was well known, the unique and troublesome layout, especially the elevator in the middle of the building and a water main we'd later discover in the middle load bearing wall, posed challenges.

Ultimately we were a destination.

***

We designed three areas for dining:

Celebration, the main dining room with Struggle-Liberation mural on the east wall chronicling the LGBT movement over the last 100 years (including victories and setbacks) with the following from Tony Kushner's "Angels in America: "The disease may be the end of us, but not nearly all and the dead will be commemorated and will struggle on with the living. AND WE ARE NOT GOING AWAY. We will not die secret deaths anymore. The world only spins forward. We will be citizens. The time has come. The Great Work Begins."

The Famous 50 mural on the north side. Although we couldn't actually bring the famous LGBTs together who inspired Out On Main, we could bring them together in this mural.

CAPABLE OF BETRAYAL

Intimacy, the second dining area in the middle of the restaurant with smaller tables and comfortable built-in banquettes. Candlelit most evenings, a quiet space for romantics and first dates.

Gathering, the third dining area, had a community vibe to it. Couches made it nice and cozy. Each table had a glass top shadow box, each box telling a short story from LGBT history. Windows faced south and a showcase with a Liberace costume along the middle hallway wall.

In the showcases that separated Intimacy from Celebration and Gathering were a signed Melissa Etheridge guitar and Greg Louganis speedo.

The piano bar was the site of impromptu and planned performances. Ann Hampton Calloway performed multiple times. Eartha Kitt and cast from The Wiz sang around our piano bar, including small size actors and actresses who played the Munchkins, and a then unknown Peter Dinklage. At the end of the evening, with it storming outside, I loaded about five munchkins into the back boot of my SUV, ten eyes staring up at me, and honestly I tried not to laugh but then they laughed at the wondrous absurdity of it and we had a good laugh together. At their hotel entrance, I lifted each one up from the boot and placed each on the ground, one at a time. You think as a restauranteur you've seen and done it all, and then this. Adorable and a once-in-a-lifetime unique experience for sure.

Also local talent were welcome to sing and play at Out On Main's piano bar.

(One Sunday evening, when I was tallying receipts for the previous week, I received a phone call and a familiar voice came on the line: "Mr. Michael Caven...this is Eartha Kitt. I loved your Weiner Schnitzel the other night. Can you bring me a serving? I'm at the Southern Hotel." Of course I was happy to do so. Eartha invited me to sit with her and chat while she dined on her favorite Schnitzel plus our popular Sweet Potato Bisque. "I'm surprised your restaurant isn't in a bigger city," she remarked. I replied that I'm not sure it would be as successful. She added: "The big mural in your dining room. It got my attention." She teared up. "I lost so many friends to AIDS." I thanked her for being such a strong advocate for the gay community. "My gays are my people," she said.)

**

An annual celebrity visit to Out On Main was Betty DeGeneres. In the 1990's, Ellen's mom Betty traveled the USA as an LGBT-ally. Her visits to Out On Main were fun, and she'd always say, "Someday I'm going to bring Ellen!"

We couldn't wait!!!

And that day eventually arrived, on Betty's 70th birthday, May 20, 2000.

Ellen was in town with her reboot concert at The Palace Theatre. "Where would you like to have your birthday dinner?" she asked her mom. "I've got the perfect place," Betty responded.

Ellen called *Out On Main* directly to make a reservation for 20, her entire posse. "Oh Hi Ellen! " JP our manager said when he picked up the phone, not missing a beat. (JP had started out as a part-time server, then onto head server, banquet manager and eventually GM. I was proud of all our team members' development and progress.)

I've played many roles at Out On Main. Being a bodyguard was a first, and I was up for the task.

Ellen and Betty, then partner Anne Hecht and the entire production crew descended on Out On Main after Ellen's show. As did many fans and groupies and the rest.

That leads us to the bodyguard part.

After getting Ellen's 20 person entourage settled, I found I needed to be standing behind Ellen, Anne and Betty and dissuade well-wishers to give our special guests time to enjoy their meals and post-show excitement.

Everyone seemed to understand and dinner carried on without incident.

Afterward Ellen and crew were gracious—posing for pictures and signing autographs. I took Ellen on a tour of the restaurant and she told me she considered opening an LGBT themed cafe in Los Angles after she came out years earlier.

I am actually touring icon Ellen DeGeneres through our little restaurant in the Midwest!!!

Ellen asked if I could find a pianist—she wanted to sing Happy Birthday to Betty. I sent for the pianist who was playing downstairs at Club Diversity. Unaware of our special guests, the surprised and overwhelmed piano player Tom Crumley arrived to our happening upstairs.

The entire restaurant sang Happy Birthday to Betty while the piano player hit the notes and kept shaking his unbelieving head.

A magical evening, indeed.

One more celebrity story.

Years earlier as a lost 13-year-old, I would play hooky from school and watch TV. In addition to Farmer's Daughter and Green Acres, a favorite show was the PTL Club. As I shared earlier in this book, I'd take my mom's Valium and watch Tammy Faye Bakker carry on like the crazy white woman she was, crying for the same reason (Valium) that Tammy Faye (Valium) was.

Imagine my excitement years later with news that Tammy Faye would be arriving to Columbus as a special guest of the Red Party, the first and original gay circuit party franchise in the US. And ahead of the party, dinner at Out On Main!

Yet again, patrons at Out On Main were surprised and delighted with another special gay icon guest. When I took Tammy Faye to tables for introductions the looks on people's faces ranged from shock to absolute giddiness.

"This is really Tammy Faye at my table, not a drag queen!" one regular remarked.

As with Ellen, I took Tammy Faye on a tour of Out On Main. She was especially impressed with the Liberace outfit.

"I watched you as a teenager, Tammy Fay," I told her.

I told Tammy about my teenage Valium trips while viewing hers and Jim Bakker's PTL Club.

"Honey, you weren't alone," she said. "I've heard this from others!"

She stopped, looked into my eyes: "No Valium today!" I nodded enthusiastically.

I pulled out a picture when I dressed up as Tammy Faye in Washington D.C. "Very nice," she said. "But honey, everybody wants to be me, but there's only me...I am the real Tammy Faye!"

"Tammy, I have to ask: Who loves me?"

With her trademark smile, the one I'd watched over and over so many years ago, she said: "God loves you. He really does."

Although not religious anymore, I certainly felt the Power of Tammy Faye Bakker that evening!

Crazy dreams do come true, after all.

Our Out On Main Restaurant regulars included solo acts—folks who were single and became a part of our living mosaic.

As much as I enjoyed our celebrities, I cherished our solo acts as I knew how important we were in their lives and they in ours.

The Sapphire Club—a group of cross-dressers, mostly heterosexual men who later in life were coming to terms with—or exploring—their gender identities—would meet privately in our banquet room—because they felt safe. We arranged make-up artists and fashion guides as most of these courageous yet cautious men had little experience with female grooming and wardrobe.

Featured on CNN International and locally, Tom and I became the "IT Gay Couple" in Central Ohio. It made us happy knowing that younger LGBTs would read (or watch) stories about us and the restaurant.

Activists and authors visited when in town. Open Book, an LGBT themed bookstore in the Short North (in and of itself a community hub), sent every book signing author, including Sapphire, comedienne Bob Smith and more.

One Saturday evening I heard a yelp from a table and rushed over. The patron just realized that his favorite author Allan Gurganus was sitting at the next table.

We called these *happenings.*

Every weekend and frequently during quieter times we'd experience happenings of some kind: proposals, coming outs (including the 75-year-old father of longtime friend Denise), birthdays and anniversaries. We were quite popular with higher profile heterosexual couples who were having affairs—they felt it was unlikely they'd be recognized at our restaurant.

Indeed the Out On Main mission, vision and promise was a great story. We delivered great food and service. I trained my team that mistakes happen and are OK; fixing them in real time is the key so patrons leave happy. That approach worked well for all of us. I worked tables after each sitting: some patrons like longer chats, others a quick hello. Give them what they want. Chef worked tables too in his whites and Chef's toque (white hat) but I suspect perhaps at times he was scanning for a date.

But we'd have to be creative to stay in the media spotlight.

We did this with theme dinner parties.

First up, and certainly the splashiest, was our Titanic Dinner. Announced in tandem with the movie's Oscar nominations (and covered by all local media), our black-tie dinner sold-out in 24 hours. Chef Don recreated the final 14-course meal served on Titanic. We did a design refit with Titanic images, artifacts and chandeliers. A few patrons showed up with life preservers. And like a well oiled machine, we delivered a Titanic-sized evening, but without a shipwreck.

(A week later there was a water leak from an upper floor and water cascaded along the restaurant public bathroom hallway walls— would have been perfect on the big night, we lamented!)

The following year was Orient Express dinner with lush visuals and high fashion.

To bring in the Millennium--New Years Eve 2000--we recreated Versailles and a French menu inspired by famous historical Versailles dinner parties.

We also had fashion shows, every kind of imaginable fundraiser in our banquet space, commitment ceremonies and weddings.

One day I received a call from a community activist with the local chapter of the Human Rights Campaign (HRC).

"We'd like to honor you and Tom with this year's HRC Equality Award," he said.

I was complemented and taken back, this was far beyond an earlier received Living Legend award.

"Seems like kind of soon," I responded. "We have a lot more activism ahead."

"Yes but the timing and significance of yours and Tom's impact on the Columbus LGBT community makes this the perfect time for you both to receive the Equality Award."

Tom and I were indeed honored and agreed.

HRC is the premier national LGBT rights organization in the US. Annual HRC black-tie dinners take place in major US cities. I remember the first HRC dinner I attended in Dallas with Frank many years earlier. It was an empowering experience to hear great speeches and news about next steps in the expansion of rights for LGBT people.

My beloved Granchar would travel from Marianna to Columbus for the big night.

To be honest, the whole thing was a dream come true. We'd finally arrived and I'd finally gotten the respect and redemption that I'd been wanting for a long time.

When Tom and I were introduced to the HRC stage, we received a standing ovation from the crowd of 600 attendees. We made our way to the stars planted on the stage. So many years later, I was having my real "Here's Johnny" moment and standing on a star that Granchar and I have talked about and dreamed about so many years earlier in Marianna when watching "The Tonight Show."

I didn't want the applause to end. But when it did, Tom and I kissed and gave our speeches. He thanked his parents and family; I thanked Granchar, introduced her and like a pro she stood up and waved during the applause.

Granchar and I looked at each other and smiled.

We'd done it!

And to add icing on the cake, Hollywood Icon Judith Light was the keynote speaker that evening.

We chatted afterward and she said to me and Tom, "You're the two who kissed. That was so sweet! The best moment tonight!"

Moments are not forever.

***

"Come to Marianna. Mike-o. I've got two weeks to live," Granchar said.

Although in good health much of her life, off the cigs the last 20 years, Granchar, despite working for a local physician, prided herself on never needing a doctor visit for her entire life and living as she pleases thanks to "sociable" security, as she liked to call it.

Granchar seemed slower a few months earlier when we met in New York City for the GLAAD Awards.

Although saddened with the news, I wasn't surprised and made my way, with Tom and his mom Annie, for Granchar's final bow.

And it did not disappoint. She was in rare form when we arrived.

"It'll be a good death, Mike-o!" she exclaimed. "And no radiation treatments so I won't be bald in heaven!"

CAPABLE OF BETRAYAL

Granchar had pictures out on the coffee table of our travels together as well as her niece and nephews. The previous year I'd taken Granchar on a Mediterranean cruise. (Of all of my mistakes with family, I was grateful that I got this one right.)

Late one night, perhaps mellow on the painkillers, Granchar disclosed her affair with actress Ann B Davis of the Brady Bunch. Ms. Davis was traveling with a summer stock company through the south, and stayed in the front bedroom of Granchar's home, until she moved to Granchar's bed. "We'd write to each other," Granchar shared. "Then the letters stopped," as Granchar blew her nose and wiped away a tear.

And in fact, it was a kind and merciful passing, perfect for the Southern Lady that Granchar was.

On Granchar's death bed, surrounded by me and adult nieces and nephews, her favorite singer Pavarotti's "Nessun Dorma" playing in the background, she lifted her arms at one point.

"Can you see them?" I asked.

Granchar's eye moistened, she nodded and reached her arms further outward and up.

"Go," I said. "They're waiting for you. We love you always."

A tiny tear made its way down her cheek. By the time it dropped off her face, my beloved Granchar was gone, her hair turning its final shade of bright white.

To where, who knows? But it was a happy and peaceful ending.

At the memorial service at St Luke's Episcopal Church in Marianna, a dozen friends and family spoke about the many ways "Our Charlotte" positively impacted the lives of regular folk.

And not-so-regular.

One person stepped forward. There was silence as the speaker was obviously transgender.

"With Miss Charlotte, I found acceptance," she said. "We had many chats on her front porch, and it wasn't just me. Her Pink Flamingos on the front lawn attracted us. We all knew we could get a fair hearing from Miss Charlotte. She wouldn't judge us and asked many questions about our lives. Most important, she encouraged me to be myself. To be proudly myself. And I did. Thank you, Miss Charlotte and fly with the angels, sweetheart."

My own personal monsters persist.

Tom and I part ways after bringing the curtain down on Out On Main.

Life would go on and take me to Philadelphia.

A while later, Tom was in DC for a conference and came to Philly afterward.

"Mikey, I've met the one," he said with a big smile and eyes sparkling with all the possibilities that lay ahead.

"His name is Rick. I think he's going to be the next love of my life."

And so began a new adventure for Tom. He and Rick would marry and start a family.

I'd eventually make it to the other side of the world and a full and productive life in Vietnam.

Like my parents Maribeth and Fred, who were longtime high school teachers, like my teacher Larry Lane Bateman, I'd become a teacher as well, a highly respected business communication specialist at the University of Da Nang in Vietnam.

About writing in Vietnam:

Come to Vietnam to write your memoir. The words will fall out of the sky and onto your iPad, sometimes as hail, sometimes as drizzle, sometimes as thunder and lightning. But the words, they will come…often when you least expect them and most need them.

Some final thoughts as my "Coming of Sage" memoir comes to a close.

I've been looking over my shoulder a lot in these pages, looking at the younger drunken, abused, desperate selves of the past. At the beginning this journey I mentioned a banquet of stars. The stars in my orbit are my best allies and teachers and icons; the amazing times I've lived, survived and thrived; all sitting at the table together with gratitude, peace and hope for the future.

In 2024 I wrote in the New Hampshire Union Leader: *This I can assert joyously: Life can improve after abuse. The challenge for the male survivor is to find and accept the compassion they deserve, even if it is missing from those who might be expected to step forward. And for everybody else, there's an obligation: to explore our own thinking, until we can fully accept the reality of male sexual abuse and deal with its consequences.*

CAPABLE OF BETRAYAL

Perhaps all this is new to you? Thank you for reading with an open heart and mind.

If you've been victimized and are on the road to recovery, remember:

We survived; now we thrive.

For those who've been keeping it all inside, remember: any day is a good day to talk about it – avail yourself of trusted friends, therapist, family.

You are worth recovery and healing. .

Acknowledgements

First, to Tin my partner, my deepest appreciation to you and the life we share.

To Tom, our ten years are always with me; you never gave up on me; I am grateful.

To Enzo, a lifelong love.

Andrea, your Claudia Schiffer legs continue to amaze.

To all my Vietnamese friends, colleagues and amazing students, too numerous to note but in my heart always.

Back in the day, Arnie Huftalen, federal prosecutor who treated me with respect and dignity, and understood why I held Bateman to account.

Granchar, my Auntie Mame, rest-in-peace or the nearest gay bar up there, miss you every day.

Scott, we were broke students, now we're doing pretty well. You accepted and loved me no matter what.

If I didn't mention you here but we shared the journey somewhere along the way, thank you and see you again…somewhere…somehow.

www.ingramcontent.com/pod-product-compliance
Lightning Source LLC
Chambersburg PA
CBHW010935120626
46552CB00010B/3262